CBT MADE SIMPLE

12 Practical Strategies to Overcome Depression, Anger, and Anxiety and Finally Manage Your Worries

© **Copyright 2019 by Clement Hawk**
All rights reserved.

This eBook is provided with the sole purpose of providing relevant information on a specific topic for which every reasonable effort has been made to ensure that it is both accurate and reasonable. Nevertheless, by purchasing this eBook you consent to the fact that the author, as well as the publisher, are in no way experts on the topics contained herein, regardless of any claims as such that may be made within. As such, any suggestions or recommendations that are made within are done so purely for entertainment value. It is recommended that you always consult a professional prior to undertaking any of the advice or techniques discussed within.

This is a legally binding declaration that is considered both valid and fair by both the Committee of Publishers Association and the American Bar Association and should be considered as legally binding within the United States.

The reproduction, transmission, and duplication of any of the content found herein, including any specific or extended information will be done as an illegal act regardless of the end form the information ultimately takes. This includes copied versions of the work both physical, digital and audio unless express consent of the Publisher is provided beforehand. Any additional rights reserved.

Furthermore, the information that can be found within the pages described forthwith shall be considered both accurate and truthful when it comes to the recounting of facts. As such, any use, correct or incorrect, of the provided information will render the Publisher free of responsibility as to the actions taken outside of their direct purview. Regardless, there are zero scenarios where the original author or the Publisher can be deemed liable in any fashion for any damages or hardships that may result from any of the information discussed herein.

Additionally, the information in the following pages is intended only for informational purposes and should thus be thought of as universal. As befitting its nature, it is presented without assurance regarding its prolonged validity or interim quality. Trademarks that are mentioned are done without written consent and can in no way be considered an endorsement from the trademark holder.

Table of Contents

SECTION I: COGNITIVE BEHAVIORAL THERAPY 1

INTRODUCTION 2

CHAPTER 1: UNDERSTANDING WHEN THERAPY IS BENEFICIAL 6

    When to Seek Therapy 10

        Anger 10

        Anxiety 12

        Depression 13

CHAPTER 2: WHAT IS COGNITIVE BEHAVIORAL THERAPY? 16

CHAPTER 3: KEY TERMS AND CONCEPTS IN CBT 24

    Automatic Thoughts 24

    Cognitive Distortions 28

    Cognitive Restructuring 30

    Core Beliefs 31

    Emotional Triggers 33

CHAPTER 4: HOW CBT WORKS 36

SECTION II: 12 CB STRATEGIES FOR OVERCOMING DEPRESSION, ANGER, AND ANXIETY 45

CHAPTER 5: INTRO TO STRATEGIES IN CBT 46

    Strategy 1: Journaling 52

        Identifying Core Beliefs through Journals 53

        Tracking Emotional Triggers through Journals 55

    Strategy 2: Creating and Reciting Affirmations 59

        What is an affirmation? 59

How to create an affirmation...60

How to use an affirmation 63

Strategy 3: Identifying and Challenging Cognitive Distortions...70

Types of Cognitive Distortions 70

Strategy 4: Worst Case Scenario Roleplay..........................85

Strategy 5: Exposure Therapy 93

Strategy 6: Challenging Negative Thoughts....................102

Negative Thought Activity..103

Can I prove my thought with substantial evidence? 104

Can I disprove my thought? 105

Am I jumping to conclusions without seeing the whole picture? 106

What would my friend/family member/significant other think about this thought and situation?.........107

How does my situation change if I look at it positively instead of negatively? 108

Will this situation triggering my negative thought still be relevant in a year?...108

One Negative Thought, Two Positive Thoughts............109

Strategy 7: Setting Goals...111

Why Set Goals?...111

Bad Goals..112

SMART Goals...114

Examples of Goals..119

Strategy 8: Mindful Meditation...120

Strategy 9: Thought-Feeling-Action Charts 127

- Identifying your Thought-Feeling-Action Cycles... 128
- Creating New Thought-Feeling-Action Cycles 130
- Strategy 10: Create an Action Plan...................................... 134
  - What Makes a Good Action Plan?.................................. 135
  - How to Make an Action Plan 135
  - Benefits of Action Plans... 139
- Strategy 11: Self-Care.. 141
  - What Self-Care Entails 141
  - Physical Self-Care.. 142
  - Psychological Self-Care.. 143
  - Emotional Self-Care.. 144
  - Relationship Self-Care... 145
  - Create a Self-Care Plan.. 146
- Strategy 12: Find a Good Therapist 150
  - Qualities of a Good Therapist... 151
  - How to Find and Choose a Therapist 156
- CONCLUSION 160

SECTION I:
COGNITIVE BEHAVIORAL THERAPY

INTRODUCTION

Do you sometimes feel depressed? Like life keeps going on around you, but you fail to see the point in anything? Or maybe you feel like an angry person, constantly on a short fuse and unable to control when you explode. Are you anxious on a regular basis to the point where you are starting to feel as if you will never be able to enjoy life to its fullest due to your fears? Have you tried to deal with these problems in the past, but found yourself lost, unsure where to start? Did you hit a roadblock you could not figure out how to surpass? No matter where you are on your journey toward solving your own problem, *CBT Made Simple* is here to help.

CBT stands for cognitive behavioral therapy. This is a type of therapy that has been proven to be incredibly efficient at altering your thought processes in a process called cognitive restructuring, and with that process, you are able to change your behaviors. In theory, this can be used to fix any thoughts that are causing you behavioral issues and can be used for mental health issues such as depression, anxiety, or anger management. Each of these can be daunting to handle on their own, but with the assistance of CBT, you will be able to take control of your thoughts, and your life, once and for all.

This book will provide you with the understanding of cognitive behavioral therapy at its core, so you learn how the processes work and understand that everything this book will guide you through is deliberate. You will be guided through the key concepts to CBT, as well as how it works. Once you are armed with the knowledge of why and how you will be provided with twelve distinct strategies and activities to use to cope with and overcome your mental health issues.

Before we get started, it is important to note that this book is not a replacement for a therapist; you will never get the same level of insight from a book as you would be seeing a therapist who can tailor all conversations and interactions to your specific situation and personality. However, this is a great stepping stone to delve into helping yourself if you feel you are not yet ready for a therapist, or you have some sort of obstacle preventing you from seeing a therapist regularly.

If you ever feel like your feelings are too overwhelming, or you are thinking of harming yourself or others, please do not hesitate to contact your local emergency services for aid, or contact a trusted friend or family member to send aid. These feelings are considered an emergency, and your local services will usually be able to help stabilize you and keep you safe, no matter what your ability to pay is. There is absolutely no shame in seeking the help you need, no matter what anyone around you may say. You deserve to live a life happy and free from constant stress, anger, fear, or hopelessness. You can get that life with perseverance and tenacity, even if it means seeking help from outside sources.

CBT MADE SIMPLE

Thank you again for choosing this book and if you liked it, I would be happy to know what you think about leaving a brief review on Amazon

CHAPTER 1: UNDERSTANDING WHEN THERAPY IS BENEFICIAL

Therapy has developed quite a stigma in the past. People assume that therapy is only for people that are so broken, they can't help themselves, or they are too weak to pull themselves up by their bootstraps and keep trekking forward. However, what these people typically don't realize is that that expression has been corrupted over time, and the meaning is now the opposite of what was intended. It is literally impossible to pick yourself up by your bootstraps, no matter how hard you may try, and yet it is a common phrase meaning get up and force something to happen. Just as it is impossible to lift yourself by your bootstraps, some people find it impossible just to pick themselves up and get moving past depression, anxiety, or anger. These issues can be debilitating to people under their influence, and no amount of telling them to try harder will fix their problems.

This is where therapy comes in. Therapy can provide plenty of insight to why we behave the way we do, as well as provide us with new ways to behave in more productive ways. It teaches us how to unpack and cope with overwhelming feelings, and gives us someone to speak to, uncensored and unafraid of judgment. The skills you can learn from a good therapist are invaluable, and too many people underestimate just how valuable it can be.

Nearly every person in this world could benefit from therapy, and those who would not typically have some other underlying disorder that would prevent it from being useful. For example, people diagnosed with narcissistic personality disorder typically believe that they are superior to everyone and always right, so they struggle to admit fault or believe that they need any sort of help to change who they are. Therapy almost always fails for these people due to their personality disorders, but most people, regardless of whether they have a debilitating mental health issue or not. Everyone can learn something from therapy, even if it is just learning coping mechanisms or understanding where an interaction went wrong.

While therapy can be an invaluable asset, it is not necessarily required every time something bad happens in life. Plenty of people manage to cope with stressors and traumatic events just fine without requiring therapy. They have developed an arsenal of coping mechanisms that help them, and after a period of time, they are able to return to life as if it had not just been disrupted. This can most often be imagined as someone whose mother has just passed away. You expect the person to be upset about losing his mother for a long while. However, most people are able to get through their grief and eventually return back to their old life. While he may always miss his mother and will undoubtedly be overwhelmed by his sadness sometimes, he by and large can get through his day just fine. He was likely taught ways to manage his feelings when growing up, and is able to rationalize that yes, he is upset about losing his mother, but that is the natural order of the world, and as much as he hates it, he knows she is no longer in any pain or suffering, and he knows she loved him dearly.

Sometimes, however, people absolutely need therapy to be able to get through something. If the man whose mother passed away was unable to function for an extended period of time due to his grief and finds himself unable to enjoy even the most basic hobbies and interests, he had before, he would most likely benefit by seeking outside help or learning new skills to help him cope. Grief, while it often never fully goes away, usually becomes easier to live with over time as you reach acceptance for what has happened. When this never happens, you may need further help to get to that point.

Likewise, if you feel as if your anxiety is hindering you to the point you are unable to function or do things you enjoy, it is time to evaluate whether you need help. If your feelings are negatively impacting your life to the point of misery, or are causing issues for others around you as they try to accommodate your own issues or insecurities, seeking help is a valid strategy.

You deserve to live your life without constant fear, depression, or anger shadowing every aspect. You deserve to be able to live the life you want, work toward goals, and enjoy your hobbies without mental health issues getting in your way. If therapy is what it will take to get yourself to that baseline, then you should welcome it with open arms.

When to Seek Therapy

Anger

Anger is a normal emotion we all feel relatively regularly in a reaction to feeling threatened. Anger on its own can be constructive and helpful as an emotion; it allows people to assert themselves and get what they need while also allowing them to protect themselves.

Evolutionarily, it is a defense mechanism to help animals fight for their lives to survive, and while we are no longer typically in situations where our very lives are at risk, we do still feel that instinctual drive to protect ourselves when we feel wronged or threatened. Our brains react strongly, even if the threat happens to be someone telling you your work is incompetent or insulting you, and for people with a particularly strong fight instinct, they will be quick to anger.

This anger can quickly become a problem, however, when it starts becoming unreasonable. If simple day-to-day annoyances can send you spiraling into a rage, you may have an anger management problem. Your body has become so accustomed to using anger to solve problems that it is your first line of defense. Before trying to defuse a situation or solve it through legitimate means, your instinct is to lash out and solve it through brute force. The physical and verbal violence you resort to causes deep scars in your relationships, and seriously hinder your ability to carry on a normal life. No one deserves to live life with an abuser, and you will find many people avoiding you if your anger outbursts become out of control. When people around you are actively telling you, your reactions are a problem or you recognize that your reactions are disproportionate to the perceived crime, it may be time to seek help with anger management.

Anxiety

Like anger, anxiety is a natural, normal emotion in moderation. This emotion is an evolutionary tool for motivating survival: When in a state of anxiety, your senses are heightened, you are aware of more of what is going on around you, and you feel hypervigilant. While this can be normal and healthy in extreme situations where vigilance will keep you alive, such as an ancient human returning to his tribe after dark after a hunting expedition, it can be debilitating if it becomes chronic.

For some people, they feel constantly anxious, as if their very lives are constantly under threat of attack, but they do not know from where or when. They spend their time afraid of some unseen force, never able to truly relax and rest. This can very quickly spiral into physical symptoms, feeling heart palpitations, or a sense of disaster, and all of the anxiety's symptoms can manifest so strongly that sufferers sometimes struggle to function at all. Constantly crippled by the fear of something happening, they find themselves unable to do anything.

Depression

Depression is a commonly misunderstood mental health issue. So many people see it as weakness or unwillingness to do better, but this is completely inaccurate. People with depression are not weak or unwilling; they simply do not see the point in trying. Oftentimes, life has beaten them down so much that they cannot see the positives in life. They lose the ability to feel pleasure for the things they once loved to do. They lose their very motivated to continue and slowly withdraw away from everything around them. As they lose their ability to feel positive, they lose their ability to regulate their moods, and as a result, all of the key social behaviors humans have developed over time are lost.

When feeling less positive, people are less likely to engage in helpful behavior with others. By not helping, they are not developing a loyalty relationship with others in their social groups. By not being positive, people with depression also struggle to engage in critical thinking, which oftentimes leaves them stuck in a negative mindset and not seeing any real solution to the problem. This leaves the person with depression spiraling into a cycle of not feeling motivated to do anything, or feeling as if he or she cannot do anything, and then not doing anything, which further worsens the mood, which exacerbates the entire problem. This loop becomes incredibly difficult to remove oneself from on his or her own, and when stuck in that loop, seeking therapy is always a wonderful option. Whether engaging in the steps on your own or seeking a trained professional, the therapeutic process should absolutely be pursued if you feel as if you yourself have become trapped in that loop of negativity and hopelessness.

CHAPTER 2: WHAT IS COGNITIVE BEHAVIORAL THERAPY?

Emotions are a normal part of human living: We might feel disappointed after finding out that a friend canceled plans, or angry when dealing with a particularly demanding client at work, or sad if a pet or family member passes away. Feelings are normal parts of our lives, and they have evolutionary purposes. As social creatures, intense feelings keep our social groups and us safe and cared for. Anger drives us to protect ourselves from perceived threats or challenges. Sadness at the loss of someone close to your heart is a byproduct of the deep love we feel for them that drove us to help them in life. It is completely normal to feel a wide range of feelings, and even negative feelings are healthy and beneficial to a certain extent.

Sometimes, however, the negative feelings become overwhelming and go beyond the norm. They begin to interfere with daily life, making it difficult to function. For those who cannot quite get their emotions or behaviors under control, CBT has become a valuable asset. At its core, CBT is a form of psychotherapy, meaning that it is based on talking and establishing a relationship between patient and therapist in order to see desired changes in behavior. As the name suggests, this therapy combines cognitive therapy with behavior therapy in order to take aspects of each and create an entirely new type of therapy. By taking the best of both worlds, CBT is able to change behaviors through changing thoughts and can change thoughts by changing behaviors.

Most often, CBT seeks to identify the causes or triggers of certain behaviors and teach the patient how to correct for them by intentionally changing thoughts that precede the behavior. For example, if you know that when you are feeling down on yourself, you tend to lash out at others in anger,

CBT would propose that you can eliminate lashing out at others by changing your thoughts, so you no longer feel down about yourself. Instead of feeling like you have first to address your behaviors of lashing out, and then address how you feel about yourself, CBT argues that the two are closely intertwined, and you can kill two birds with one stone by changing the thought behind the behavior. This therapy seeks to improve mental well-being in patients, correct problematic behaviors, beliefs, feelings, or compulsions, and also teach the patient how to better interact with other people to strengthen relationships and the social skills of that particular person. Through talking and interacting with the patient, the therapist is able to guide him or her through the process and toward the desired results.

CBT has four key defining factors that help the therapist accomplish helping the patient in these ways: It is goal-oriented, present-focused, active, and brief. With these guiding features, CBT teaches long-term behavioral changes in a short period of time. It has become incredibly popular in recent days for mental health care because of its effectiveness; even the United States military advocates for its use due to effectiveness and efficiency in treating mental health issues with long-term results. Ranging from anxiety and depression to more serious forms of mental illness, such as psychosis or schizophrenia, CBT has been shown to be effective at mitigating mental health issue disorders and having lasting effects. This is because CBT, at its simplest, teaches people to change their thoughts, emotions, or actions on whatever triggers they identify in order to alleviate symptoms.

CBT focuses on goals due to its nature as problem-solving therapy. Since problem-solving is always easier when you have a goal of solving a specific problem, CBT is more efficient utilizing them. These goals can have an end result, such as lessening feelings of anxiety or cutting your angry outbursts in half during the week. No matter what it is in life that you strive for, CBT will be able to help guide you to that goal and help teach you proper goal-forming strategies, which will be discussed in Section II Strategy 7: Setting Goals.

This therapy focuses on the present, with the reason being that the current triggers for the behavior are much more important to understand that the reason for the behaviors, to begin with. Just as if you care more about what is broken than why when trying to fix your car, understanding what your current mental health struggles are is more important than the initial cause. By focusing on the present and looking to change reactions to certain triggers in order to mitigate the negative response, you begin to achieve your goals sooner and with a nearly permanent fix. While understanding and unpacking the trauma from the past is important, ultimately, in CBT, knowing the origins of the behavior does not necessarily allow for it to be fixed as much as knowing what the current triggers, especially since you will never be able to fix the past trauma. You can, however, fix current feelings on the trauma, which should change behaviors.

CBT focuses on active changes to your life as you live it rather than speaking about past events and hoping to make them less painful or triggering over time or avoiding the stressors that cause you problems. It is important to remember the past and cope with it, but ultimately, actively focusing on changing your behaviors and learning new techniques to help you change your current mindset is more important to see quicker results with your mental health. Rather than addressing one specific problem, you are given the tools you need to alter thinking in all aspects of your life that can be applied to any behavior you want to change. Rather than learning to cope, you are given a new way of life. Just like you can feed a man for a day with a single fish, but you can teach him to feed himself for life by giving him the skills needed to fish himself, this therapy gives you coping skills so you can handle any stressors life throws your way.

The last important aspect of CBT is that it is brief. While in many other psychotherapies, you may spend years seeing your therapist regularly before deciding you are ready to go off on your own, in CBT, you often only see the therapist a dozen times before being set out to manage your feelings on your own. Since CBT teaches you the skills you need, you do not need to stay in it for long. Once you know how to change your thoughts, it would be a waste of your time and money to repeatedly go back every time you have any sort of problem in your life.

All of these aspects combine into one incredibly effective therapy, focused on teaching you the skills you need to cope, the motivation necessary to inspire change, action plans, and making all of the above as brief as possible. These come together, working in tandem to provide the effect needed to help you rewire your brain from any kind of negative thinking and relieve distressing symptoms. With the power of CBT, you will be able to overcome nearly any distressing thoughts, feelings, or behaviors that you have felt are beginning to negatively impact your life.

CHAPTER 3: KEY TERMS AND CONCEPTS IN CBT

Before delving into CBT, you first must understand the most basic concepts and vocabulary that are used. The following concepts will come up during the process of restructuring your thoughts, and in the strategies, this book will provide you. Think of this as your translation dictionary that will break concepts into easily understood terms. This is by no means a complete list of important aspects in CBT, but it does address the ones that will be relevant to this book.

Automatic Thoughts

During the course of your day, you have more automatic thoughts than you can imagine. These can range from noticing someone's shirt color to registering when a person decides to merge into your lane while driving and you instinctively slow just enough to give the driver enough space to pass you. These automatic thoughts are snap judgments that influence your behavior without taking up your conscious thought processes. By not having to focus on these instinctive behaviors, you are free to worry about more complicated thoughts that require more cognition instead, such as worrying about your work deadline or how you will schedule your evening.

These thoughts come unbidden but are quickly ignored or forgotten, as they are hardly relevant to continue about your day. You do not think about why you need to slow down when approaching a stop light, nor do you think about how you slow down; you simply do it and continue driving. These involuntary, reactionary thoughts are your automatic thoughts. They can be neutral or somewhere on the positive or negative scale. While these thoughts are meant to be useful, sometimes, they can be skewed and become detrimental instead.

When automatic thoughts become detrimental, they are considered negative automatic thoughts. This is one of the types of thoughts that CBT seeks to correct. Negative automatic thoughts are also largely unconscious, and they color your perception of what is happening around you. These are underlying thoughts of unworthiness, uselessness, feeling as if you are unloved, or believing you are unimportant or unintelligent. These thoughts may have been internalized through past experiences, and they color your perception of everything. Any time something goes wrong, your automatic negative thought will feel justified. For example, if you take a wrong turn on your way to a new restaurant to meet someone, you might immediately tell yourself, "Wow, of course, I messed that up and missed my turn! I can't even follow my GPS right without messing something up. Now I'm late, and my friend is going to be angry." Things could have been just fine leading up to that moment, but as soon as you made a mistake, you beat yourself up over it.

That diatribe is an example of the behavior caused by an automatic negative thought. In that instance, the automatic negative thought was likely feelings of worthlessness or feeling unintelligent. The automatic negative thought is your automatic reaction of beating yourself up at any signs of perceived failure. The undertone to the thought is that you believe you are worthless, unintelligent, and unwanted. If you had told yourself, "I am stupid, and no one likes me," you would likely recognize that that is an incorrect statement, but that is the implication when you said what you did to yourself. These negative automatic thoughts can result in reacting in over-the-top fashions, such as screaming at a waiter who drops a cup, or breaking into tears because you accidentally forgot to message something silly and unimportant to a friend when you originally told her you would. CBT will teach you how to identify and correct these thoughts with a variety of different skills. For further instruction and information, see Section II: Strategy 6: Identifying and Challenging Negative Automatic Thoughts.

Cognitive Distortions

Like negative automatic thoughts, cognitive distortions are automatic thoughts, but they are distorted or patently false in some way, shape, or form. These are beliefs you may hold and take at face value, but something about them is inaccurate. Think of this like logic: If a logical argument is unsound, it is essentially worthless and can be discarded on the basis of being unsound. For example, the argument, "If I hop three times right now, then the volcano next to me will suddenly erupt. I hopped three times; therefore, the volcano is blowing up," is logically valid, meaning that the structure of the argument follows the logical rule pattern known as modus ponens. However, anyone can look at that argument and recognize that it is nonsense, even if it follows the pattern. Just as arguments can be unsound or unreasonable, so too can beliefs about the world.

These cognitive distortions can be anything from seeing your neighbor in a foul mood, and automatically deciding it is your fault. You somehow manage to rationalize the jump from point a to b, using cognitive distortions. Because your beliefs at their core are what is flawed, you have no issues accepting it quicker than you would accept the nonsense argument about hopping and volcanoes erupting. It fits the very logical pattern you have developed and fits into your argument, so you see no reason to give it a second thought or challenge it, even if it leaves you feeling down about yourself, anxious, or angry.

These cognitive distortions can be identified, though it does require time and effort. They typically follow specific patterns or fallacies, and because of that, if you analyze your deepest core beliefs, you will begin to be able to identify which of them have become distorted. This is another of the strategies that will be discussed in Section II. See Strategy 3: Identifying and Challenging Cognitive Distortions for more information on how to identify cognitive distortions and begin to challenge them.

Cognitive Restructuring

Cognitive restructuring is the process of altering your way of thinking. CBT recognizes that thoughts, feelings, and actions are an endless cycle in which thoughts influence feelings, which influence actions, which in turn influence thoughts. Everything you do feeds into this endless cycle. CBT seeks to disrupt this cycle in order to change it. For example, imagine you are someone with an anger problem. You often think about things negatively, which keeps you in a negative mood, which causes you to lash out in anger, which only makes you think even more negatively about whatever triggered the outburst in the first place.

CBT interrupts one of those aspects, typically either thoughts or actions, which upsets the entire cycle. For example, if the cause of the angry outburst was that you disliked a restaurant that your family chose to go to for dinner, so you were already in a bad mood when you walked in the door, which contributed to your explosion, CBT would likely seek to change your negative thought. Instead of being annoyed at the restaurant, CBT would have you instead focus on the positive aspect of the event, such as going to dinner with your family and enjoying the occasion, even if the food is not your favorite. By focusing on enjoying your family, you are likely to be in a better mood, which will make you much less inclined to react explosively in anger. This cognitive restructuring is used a lot in challenging both negative automatic thoughts and cognitive distortions.

Core Beliefs

Core beliefs are the beliefs you hold about yourself. They can be either negative or positive, but they color every interaction you have with others and how you perceive the world around you. These core beliefs are largely unconscious, but they can be identified through plenty of introspection and self-reflection. These beliefs are typically developed over a long period of time, typically beginning in childhood, or through significant life events. These are typically rigid beliefs, and you will react according to them, even going so far as to unconsciously force what is happening around you to fit into the core beliefs while denying or disregarding anything that would contradict it.

For example, someone with depression may look at every negative interaction he has as a sign that he is unworthy of love, or he is worthless to everyone around him. However, he will be virtually blind to every instance of those who care about him going out of their way to show they care, such as sending him a silly text of a meme they say on the internet that they know he will appreciate or having his favorite food delivered to him on his birthday.

These core beliefs can be cognitive distortions or colored by negative automatic thoughts, and they are important to understand. Once you understand how you feel about yourself, you are able to decide whether you like how you feel. If you do, you know you are secure with yourself. If you do not, you can begin the steps of cognitive restructuring to alter them.

Emotional Triggers

Sometimes, something around us suddenly triggers an overwhelming sense of negative emotion. You could have been happily chatting with someone, and at the drop of a hat, suddenly felt your blood boiling, your pulse racing, and like you cannot decide between screaming at someone or punching them. This reaction is called being emotionally triggered. You may know during, or after the fact that your reaction is irrational and disproportionate, but despite that, you cannot control it. The best you can do is seek to understand what your emotional trigger is so you can plan a way to avoid blowing up in the future.

Emotional triggers are typically related to some sort of trauma that has caused you to internalize a strong reaction to things reminiscent of the trauma. Someone who suffered through an abusive relationship might be triggered by someone saying a common phrase if it was one the abusive partner said on a regular basis. Someone traumatized by a dog attack at a young age may be triggered by the sound of barking. Someone home from war may be triggered by loud sounds reminiscent of explosions or gunfire.

Understanding what your emotional triggers are will help you begin the process of cognitive restructuring in order to retrain yourself to be less reactive to them. If you are aware that you react negatively to people with beards that surprise you, there are methods you can use to desensitize yourself to them, so your reactions are not as strong or negative. Through a combination of cognitive restructuring and exposure to your trigger in a controlled environment, you will be able to overcome these emotional triggers and stop allowing them to rule your life.

CHAPTER 4: HOW CBT WORKS

Cognitive behavioral therapy has been found to be incredibly effective in alleviating distressing symptoms, and also in leaving lasting effects on those who choose to utilize its methods. In studies comparing CBT to other psychotherapies, along with comparing to medication taken alone without any therapeutic intervention, CBT has shown a higher rate of success for a wide range of different mental health issues. Those with depression, anger issues, anxiety disorders, PTSD, and even eating disorders, have shown high rates of alleviation of symptoms if they put effort into learning the techniques taught to them and put those techniques to good use. While medication is a legitimate form of treating any sort of chemical causes for these disorders, most people who ever discontinue medication relapse shortly after, whereas those who have completed CBT still have the skills they need after completing their course of therapy.

Now, this may sound too good to be true; how could such a relatively short therapy possibly be so effective at fixing mental health issues that can literally drive people to kill themselves or hurt others? The answer is that it gives control of the situation back to the person suffering. Oftentimes, our mental health issues stem from feelings of powerlessness or as if we are spinning out of control, and CBT aims to return the control of your mind back to yourself, rather than leaving it with your emotions. Emotions are irrational and easily swayed, so when we are ruled by emotion, we find ourselves struggling to find a stable the person learns how to understand how his or her thought process works, and just how much of a ripple effect even one small negative thought can have in nearly every aspect of life. By learning how even correcting one negative thought can create positive waves, the person learns to correct negativity throughout his or her life. The end result leaves a person coping with stress better than ever, leading to a drastic reduction in stress, depression, anger, anxiety, and any other symptoms that needed changing. This leaves the individual happier and more able to take on life.

By empowering yourself with the knowledge of CBT, you make yourself self-sufficient. You learn the tools to solve your own problems on your own in ways that you can customize to your situation, and may even eliminate the need for any medication for your mental health issues. Keep in mind, however, that you should never wean yourself off of your medication without your doctor's guidance. Always seek medical advice before altering your medication regimen in any way, and remember that there is no shame in taking it if that is what keeps you sane. Ultimately, the most important part is that you are happy, healthy, and comfortable in your own mind, no matter how you get there. While CBT is incredibly effective, it does not work for everyone, and for some, medication will still be required.

CBT, despite being short and structured, has plenty of weapons in its arsenal. When seeing a therapist, he or she will be able to cater specifically to your personality and make sure that you learn the skills and complete the activities that will be the most helpful to you. When attempting CBT techniques on your own, however, you do not have the added benefit of having a professional who has experience in teaching you. Despite that, you are still able to choose whichever strategies you think may be best for you. This book will provide 12 strategies for treating CBT, and ultimately, it is up to you, which you think will work for you.

If you do engage in therapy with a skilled professional, you can expect your sessions to be short and structured. Despite the brevity, the structure maximizes the benefit to you. Typically, the beginning of the session is addressing any concerns you may have had during the time since your last session has ended, as well as reflecting on whatever assignment you were given to practice during the week. You then begin to learn a new skill that will be useful for you, followed by practicing your skills in a controlled environment with the therapist. You are then given the assignment to complete before meeting once again before you are sent on your way.

By having an assignment that requires you to use the skills taught to you during the week in real time, in real life situations, you are able to really reinforce their use in your life. As the skills taught prove themselves effective, you then use those skills more often, which gives you more benefits and positive reinforcement, which leads you to use them even more. This positive reinforcement cycle really affirms that the therapy process is working while also making waves in your life.

Just think; one tiny negative thought can derail your entire day, just like a single stone tossed into the water can ripple out to affect water quite a distance away from it. Now imagine, instead of just a pebble of a negative thought, you pick up a fistful of positive thoughts and behaviors turned into rocks and throw them into the water. It will make a much larger effect and will be much more noticeable. Those big waves are what you create as you utilize the skills taught in therapy in real time to be compliant with therapy.

This, in part, is one of the reasons CBT is so effective. You are literally tasked with changing thoughts behaviors in real time and taught the skills to do so rather than spending your time dwelling on the past to eventually try to come to terms with whatever has happened in your past. As you begin to utilize the skills and find them effective, your therapist is able to walk you through why the process worked in the first place, leaving you with a thorough understanding of how your mind works. This leaves you understanding the changes in your life at a fundamental level, which leaves you much more likely to continue including them in your life in various aspects. If you discover that repeating affirmations helped you overcome your crippling anxiety by helping you remain grounded during an exam, you may decide to try implementing them when you are stressed about a big deadline at work, or to stop yourself from lashing out at people when you are upset. Likewise, if grounding techniques worked when you felt overwhelmingly angry, you may try using them when you feel other overwhelming feelings as well. As these skills and techniques build upon themselves, they inspire you to continue making changes, and you end up with a domino effect. One change leads to another, then another and another, until you barely recognize the life you are living now but in a good way. The changes that will happen will seem almost too good to be true, but they are entirely possible if you put in the dedication.

Without a therapist to guide you, this process is a little bit different. There will not be anyone trained to help you or bounce ideas off of, nor is there anyone who can walk you through the steps and explain why things work. You have a book telling you what to do, but unable to provide real-time feedback to help you better if it is necessary. You have a cookie cutter assignment designed to help the general public, and you have to tweak it to make it specific to you and your situation. This does not mean it is impossible. However, if it were, this book would be pointless! You absolutely can attempt CBT on your own since the process itself is so relatively simple and action-based, if you have the dedication and fortitude to do so. However, if at any point, it is too much for you to handle, you should absolutely seek out professional help.

With a book, you are given an understanding of what CBT entails, as well as key concepts. You are also guided through a handful of strategies and assignments to complete that are provided. It is up to you to keep up with the work, and up to you to make sure the assignments you complete are beneficial to you. So long as you are self-driven, this process will most likely be entirely doable for you on your own. Keep in mind that there are no absolutes in psychology, however, and if you do not find this process useful, keep looking for the methods that work for you, even if that means seeking therapy, speaking to a doctor about medication, or choosing an entirely different approach altogether. Both of those are valid decisions you could make to better your situation, even if they do not involve this book.

SECTION II: 12 CB STRATEGIES FOR OVERCOMING DEPRESSION, ANGER, AND ANXIETY

CHAPTER 5: INTRO TO STRATEGIES IN CBT

Congratulations! You have made it through Section I of the book and to the section where the real work begins. This section will provide you with activities similar to the ones you would encounter in CBT with a therapist, but modified so you can do them on your own. Each strategy provided will walk you through crucial information, seeking to explain why parts of the strategies are important, and also how they can be used in a variety of situations. The strategies will provide you with examples of how each strategy may present, as well as a quick explanation of the desired result. They provide you with the ins and outs you will need to be successful as you attempt to reprogram your mind at a fundamental level.

When attempting CBT on your own, you should seek to develop an understanding of why and how

CBT works, which if you have been paying attention thus far, you already have! If not, feel free to revisit the previous chapters as many times as necessary until you are certain you understand them. Highlight sections of the text you find helpful, take notes, talk to other people about what you read, make flashcards, or do anything else that will help you learn the basic foundations of CBT. Do not hesitate to reference previous sections of the book if it will help you move forward in your process. Remember, having a good foundation of background knowledge is essential, especially when you do not have the guidance of a therapist to explain or remind you of what a certain concept is in the moment.

With that basic foundation of knowledge at your disposal and an understanding of the keywords or concepts you will encounter, you should be prepared to attempt the strategies this section. Remember, each will have to be catered to your own situation, thoughts, feelings, and problem behaviors. The activities and strategies will provide you with suggestions for ways to cater them to you, but ultimately, it will be up to you to make sure they work, and it will be up to you to make sure you stay on top of the work and activities, so you get their full benefits. Remember, with no one else holds you accountable, you have to remember to do it yourself.

Even if you are seeing an actual therapist, the strategies in this section can be beneficial as supplements for homework assignments provided in your therapy sessions. They can provide extra ways of practicing or analyzing your thoughts, which will only solidify the skills you learn in therapy. These strategies can be applied to nearly any situation by nearly any person, even if he or she does not struggle with mental health issues. Each of these new coping skills or strategies will better your life by making your thought processes healthier and focusing on being productive instead of making situations worse by reacting emotionally.

Some of these techniques compound onto themselves. For example, after learning to journal effectively and how to create affirmations, you can use both of those strategic tools to aid you in challenging cognitive distortions. Understanding how these tools can play off of one another is essential to truly understand how flexible these coping mechanisms can be. You can use your affirmations to ground yourself when practicing mindfulness, or during an action plan. You can use journaling and setting goals when practicing self-care. None of these strategies have to be taken individually and separately. Feel free to adapt these strategies and combine them further, or even discarding some of them altogether, to create a system of restructuring the mind that works best for you. Ultimately, in this process, your mind is the most important.

When trying to choose which of these strategies will be useful to you, first identify the problem you wish to solve. Are you an anxious person, or angry? Do you suffer from depression? You should then seek to highlight whichever strategies are relevant to you. All of these strategies will be of some use to anyone, but ultimately, you will have to choose the ones that really click for you. Perhaps you struggle to work through mindfulness, instead preferring to rely on affirmations and your action plans to keep control of yourself. Maybe you love to journal, but charting your actions-thoughts-feelings charts is nothing but an annoyance to you due to being simplified. Regardless of which you choose to pursue, make sure they are relevant to you, and you are fair about your standards and expectations.

Because this is so important, it will be emphasized once more: If, during this process, you ever feel as if you want to hurt yourself or others, or you have begun making a plan to end your life, please reach out to someone else immediately. Seek emergency treatment, or at the very least, reach out to a trusted individual who can help you ground yourself at the moment until you can seek treatment. These methods are successful and useful on their own, but if you are feeling urges to self-harm, you need more help than this book can provide you. Please, do what you must to stay healthy, even if that means you put this book down and seek immediate help from your local emergency room.

Strategy 1: Journaling

Journaling is not just for preteens anymore: It is a valid way to begin understanding your own subconscious thoughts, as well as for identifying your own personal core beliefs. Journals should be beneficial to you, so ultimately, you should do it in a fashion you find useful. Remember, journaling does not even necessarily have to be pen to paper: It can be in the form of recording a verbal stream of consciousness, with you speaking out loud instead of writing. You can bullet journal if you feel short on time. You can do it in the morning, afternoon, evening, or even every other day. No matter what the form your journaling takes, the most important part is that you find some sort of benefit from doing so. This strategy will provide you with two ways to journal utilizing CBT techniques: How to identify core beliefs and how to track emotional triggers.

Identifying Core Beliefs through Journals

One of the most effective ways to use a journal when attempting cognitive restructuring is to use it to identify core beliefs for later analysis. This will allow you to identify whether a belief you hold is positive, neutral, negative, or distorted in some way. This step will have you write down a strong feeling you felt at some point during the day and ask yourself what triggered the feeling.

For example, perhaps at lunch at work, your coworker you usually go to eat with left a few minutes early, causing you to completely miss running into her so you two could decide where to eat. This left you alone for lunch, feeling upset, rejected, and insecure. You would then write something along the lines of the following:

"I feel disappointed and rejected because I was left behind by Jenna at lunch today."

With the feeling identified, you should ask yourself why this is relevant. Why does feeling this way matter to you? What makes it significant or gives it power? You should then answer that question and record your answer:

"Because we always eat lunch together, but she disappeared on me."

Again, ask what the relevance of this is to your life and answer:

"Because she is probably mad at me if she doesn't want to eat lunch with me!"

Repeat this process until you reach an answer that is about yourself as opposed to an external cause or source. For example, maybe the next answer to why that is relevant is the following:

"Because I always mess things up and offend people I like."

Suddenly, you have reached the "I" statement you needed to reach in order to identify the core belief. In this case, the core belief is that you feel as if you always ruin things, or that you can never do anything right. Once you have identified your core belief, you can choose to move onto another strategy for identifying whether it is negative or distorted, or you can continue the process of identifying more of your core beliefs. We all hold dozens of them, both positive and negative, and sometimes, even pursuing the positive ones can help motivate you to keep moving forward to discover the best, healthiest you that you can be. Seeing that you have some positive core beliefs can help you through the pain or emotional distress, seeing your negative beliefs written in front of you, no longer veiled by other thoughts and feelings, can inflict.

Tracking Emotional Triggers through Journals

Another common journal tactic is to create an emotional trigger journal. This should help provide insight into exactly why you are behaving the way you are and what your most common triggers often are. First, you should identify what emotional response you want to track. This can be anything: Anger, frustration, sadness, or anything else. The goal of this journaling technique is to be able to track that emotional response to identify what triggers it. Take these one at a time as you go through the process, and recognize that sometimes, the process takes longer than you may expect.

To do this, you should carry a small notebook with you, or make sure you have a note-taking app readily available on your phone. Any time that particular emotion you want to track is starting to bubble up, you should stop yourself and write down what is happening around you that could be triggering the reaction. Include who you were interacting with, what was happening, the context, the time of day, and anything else you think is relevant to the feeling. Remember, always err on the side of recording too much information rather than not enough. You can always disregard what you write later if you decide it is irrelevant, but it is harder to remember all of the details after the fact.

Repeat this over the course of a week or two, always stopping to write down how you felt, what made you feel that way, and the context of the feeling. After that period of time, you should have several instances recorded in your journal that look something like this:

Date: 5/12 Time: 5:27 pm

Location: The office lobby at work

Feeling: Anger

What happened: I was running late to get to my son's daycare to pick him up and was certain I'd be charged an extra fee for picking him up late when I didn't have the money to pay for it. I was speed-walking to my car, but a group of people was trying to force a table through the building's doors that blocked the only exit. Their moving truck was blocking my car in, and their table was physically keeping me from leaving.

With the journal entries written in that format, you can then begin to analyze to see what is in common with all of the triggers. Is it around a mealtime? Were you hungry? Were you stressed out? What was the reason you were stressed out? Eventually, you should begin to see a pattern. Perhaps the person who was angry was stressed about money; his daycare would have charged him the money he did not have to pick up his child if he was late. He knew he didn't have money in his budget to pay for another late fee, so feeling that pressure set him off. Pair that with it being close to mealtime and him being tired after a long day of work, and of course he was easily triggered into anger. Ultimately, you should seek to identify any patterns to your emotions so you can begin to correct them with other CBT strategies, such as challenging any underlying distortions or negative thoughts or creating an action plan for the next time a similar situation arises.

Strategy 2: Creating and Reciting Affirmations

What is an affirmation?

Affirmations are incredibly useful in a wide range of life's situations. They can play a special role in cognitive restructuring, as by repeating them to yourself, you eventually begin to internalize them. They can help you ground yourself if emotions or tensions are running high, and you are unsure of how you will react. They can remind you that you are doing the right thing, even when you feel like you are not. Words have power, and the more you repeat them to yourself, the more you strengthen them.

If you have not guessed by now, an affirmation is a short phrase you tell yourself for any of the above reasons. The entire purpose of it is to remind you of something good or positive about yourself or to encourage you to keep going in a difficult situation. They are there to teach that tiny voice in the back of your mind that may have grown distorted over time that you are enough, you are worthy, and you are trying the best you can.

How to create an affirmation

You can make an affirmation for any situation, so long as it follows a basic structure. There are three rules to creating good affirmations that will serve you well: it must be present-tense, it must be focused on you, and it must be positive. With these three rules guiding you, you will be able to design and structure any number of affirmations to help you achieve the goals you are hoping to accomplish.

It must be in the present tense because then, you cannot deny it is true at that moment. You guarantee its validity to yourself at the moment if you are saying it in the present tense. If you say, "I will stop avoiding confrontation," you could argue that that only applies in the future, which gives you an out. Just like you can say, "I will start to exercise," you are not giving any sort of timeline for it, so it is plausible to deny that it is happening in the present tense. Likewise, you cannot change the past, so there is no point in focusing your affirmation on what happened before. By saying, "I am willing to engage in confrontation if necessary," you are saying that about your current self.

It must be focused on you because, in this big world, the only thing you have utter control over is yourself. You cannot control what someone else does to you, but you can control how you will react to it, and using an affirmation can help prompt you to react in a way you feel is beneficial or productive. If you were to focus it on someone else or an external force, you would have no way to guarantee or enforce it is true. You cannot say, "My friends and family will accept me for who I am" because you have no way to guarantee that. Your mind will prey on your insecurities and remind you that you cannot read their thoughts, so they could be lying to you when they say they do accept you. This is a weakness in the affirmation that will allow you to deny it, which defeats the entire purpose of the affirmation. You can, however, tell yourself, "I will take what my friends and family say about me at face value," as that is directed toward yourself.

It must be positive because the entire purpose of what you are doing is restructuring your thoughts away from negative patterns to positive ones. Consider the difference between, "I will not yell today," and "I am making an effort to keep my voice calm and respectful." You go from a negative, which still keeps your mind thinking in negatives, to a positive affirmation that gives you the instructions you need to make the change you desire to see. The difference between the two is that when you think in more positive terms, you are not making your goal avoiding something, but instead a positive action to change the situation to stop the action you no longer wish to engage in.

With these three key features, you are ready to begin the process of creating your own affirmations. Remember those three rules as you create your own, and they should be effective for you. This will be an especially useful tool in cognitive restructuring, as you can use it to disrupt thoughts or behaviors that are detrimental to your mental wellbeing.

How to use an affirmation

In order to use an affirmation, you must first create one. In order for the affirmation to be the most beneficial for you, you need to identify a problem that you seek to correct with affirmations. Do you have a specific behavior you wish to stop? Is there insecurity that always leaves you feeling vulnerable? Regardless of what the problem is, decide on what it is and write it down for yourself. Look at it and ask yourself what you can do to mitigate it.

For example, if your problem is anger and disproportionate reactions to that anger, write down what you would like to change. Are you a yeller? Or maybe you have a tendency to shut down and refuse to speak to those around you, which you know is damaging to your relationships. Identify the specific behavior, so you can create an affirmation for it. For example, with your anger issue, you might write down,

I yell too much when I get angry and it hurts those I love.

Once you have that example written down, you should think about ways to change that behavior. The obvious one is to say that you will stop yelling, but remember, stopping and avoiding behaviors are negative, and therefore are not appropriate for an effective affirmation. Instead of identifying what you should not do, seek to identify what you could do instead that will have the effect you want. Remember, CBT is active and requires positive actions rather than negative inactions, such as avoidance. Perhaps, after some careful introspection, you decide to write the following:

I can try to calm myself down when I feel mad so I do not feel the need to yell.

This is a good first step: It is focused specifically on yourself and your own actions and is half positive. It still needs some final tweaks before you are left with a polished, beautiful, effective affirmation to use to remind yourself to avoid yelling when angry. It is still a conditional statement instead of a present tense statement and is still quite vague, so that needs to be fixed next:

I am keeping my voice calm and controlled when speaking.

Now, you have a short statement that reminds you to perform an action that in turn, allows you to keep from yelling in your anger. This is a polished affirmation that has an end result that lines up with your goal. You remind yourself that you want to speak calmly when you feel angry, which prompts you to do the opposite of yelling. The first time this statement works for you, you will reinforce its usefulness, and the joy of achieving your goal of not yelling will leave you wanting to use it more and more. This positive reinforcement will be your encouragement to continue.

For the best effect, choose a few times a day that you will use to recite your affirmation to yourself at least ten times, even if you may not feel like it is relevant at that moment. The goal is for you to recite it so often that it becomes an automatic thought that influences your behavior. If you internalize that you keep your voice calm, you eventually override that initial gut reaction to yell and always default to keeping your voice calmer. You want it to become an unconscious reaction eventually, so you do not have to decide to avoid yelling consciously. For example, maybe you choose to recite the affirmation ten times as you get into your car to go to work every day, plus as you brush your teeth every night. Eventually, your mind automatically does this without effort as you get into the habit.

Affirmations for Anger

- I am in control of myself and my reactions, and I am calm even in the face of things that make me angry.
- I will speak to others with the respect I expect to receive from others.
- I am strong enough to control my anger and use those frustrating feelings in a productive manner.
- I am acknowledging my feelings of anger while maintaining control of my reactions.

Affirmations for Anxiety

- Every breath I take is giving me clarity while exhaling my fears.
- I am choosing to focus on the positives in my life to remind myself that I can live a happy life.
- I can see through the lies my anxiety feeds me and remain calm and secure in myself and my surroundings.

- I am safe at this moment, and I will remain calm.

Affirmations for Depression

- I am worthy of love and care.
- I am in control of my actions and I choose to do at least one productive thing today.
- I am strong enough to get through this, even though it is hard.
- I am actively striving to better myself and my situation.

Affirmations for Stress

- I am prepared to accept when plans change, and I am flexible enough to roll with it.
- I can handle what life is throwing at me right now, even though it is tough.
- I am strong enough to manage this stress and get through everything that is required of me and wise enough to know when I have hit my limits.

- I am allowed to take breaks when I need them.

Do you like this book? it would be important for me if I could leave a short review on amazon. thank you!

Strategy 3: Identifying and Challenging Cognitive Distortions

This strategy requires you to combine the previous two for the best results: By identifying core beliefs, you can begin to analyze them to identify where cognitive distortions lie. Once you have identified them, you are able to challenge them, which is typically done through affirmation that changes your thoughts, which change your behaviors. Please revisit Strategy 1 for information on identifying core beliefs if you have skipped it, and have your list of core beliefs in front of you for this strategy. Once you have your list of core beliefs, proceed to the next section to see if any of yours follow the patterns of various types of cognitive distortions. There are twelve cognitive distortions that this book will focus on, though some sources prefer to recognize more or less.

Types of Cognitive Distortions

Assigning Blame

Assigning guilt involves thinking in "should" or "must" forms. These thoughts tell you that things must go a certain way, and if they do not, then there is a problem somewhere. However, this can be really catastrophic, if you fail to do the things you feel you should be doing, as you suddenly blame yourself for the failure, and use that failure and blame to put yourself further down. For example, you could tell yourself that you have to write 500 words a day for a novel you have always wanted to work on so you can be finished by some arbitrary deadline you made yourself because writers can easily write 500 words in a day. If you fail to write 500 words one day, you blame yourself for failing to both meet your goal and by failing as a writer. Rather than being motivating, you find yourself feeling demotivated because you already failed once so you are doomed to continue to do so.

Catastrophizing

Catastrophizing involves assuming the worst-case scenario will always happen. For example, if your spouse is late for work, instead of assuming traffic is bad, as most reasonable people will do, someone with a tendency to catastrophize instead decides that clearly, his or her spouse got into a devastating car crash and is dead somewhere. This thinking is clearly not rational or realistic, and anyone looking at the situation would recognize the flaw in that reasoning, but to the person with the catastrophizing mindset, they seem completely reasonable.

Dichotomous Thinking

When you engage in dichotomous thinking, you see things entirely in black and white. There is no room for grey areas in this kind of thinking; it is either true, or it is false. This forces you to think in extremes, where you almost always look at the negative sides as affirming your way of thinking. This also sets you up for failure when suddenly, even a 98% score on a test is a failure because you did not get a perfect score. Because things are either black or white, less than perfect is always a failure. These are typically thoughts that begin in

"Always," "Every," "Never," or other absolute words. For example, you may have a cognitive distortion of, "I always hurt everyone I love," "Every time I attempt something important, I fail," or, "I am never missed when I don't go to group gatherings."

Emotional Reasoning

Emotional and rational are opposites for a reason: One makes judgments based on emotions while the other looks with logic. Emotional reasoning combines the two, using your emotions to justify your cognitive distortion. For example, you feel anxious about something and use that feeling of anxiety to justify the thought that something bad must be coming. Or perhaps you have made a mistake and feel incompetent at your job, so you use that feeling of incompetence or embarrassment to confirm to yourself that you are incompetent or worthless. The problem with this, however, is that feelings are irrational sometimes. Something that makes you happy today could make you feel sad tomorrow, and your feelings are constantly in a state of fluctuation. Because of this, justifications and decisions should not be made solely on emotion. Just because you feel stupid after making a mistake does not mean you are stupid, and just because you feel anxious does not mean something bad will happen. Oftentimes, these negative feelings just breed more of themselves, and dwelling on them makes it worse. You feel anxious, so you tell yourself something bad is coming, which only serves to make yourself even more anxious, which is further proof of foreboding, and this cycle continues ad nauseam.

Focusing on the Negative

Focusing on the negative is as straightforward as it sounds: You get so caught up in negative things happening that you completely miss when something good has happened. This is similar to dichotomous thinking, but there is never a positive to it. You literally always focus solely on the negative. For example, if you get into an argument with your spouse, you may immediately internalize it as a sign that your relationship is doomed to fail. This is most likely not the case; people in relationships argue or disagree sometimes. However, you get so caught up in the moment that you do not see that shortly after the argument, your spouse made your favorite meal for dinner, or complimented you when you walked by. Instead, you dwell on that one fight, seeing it as a guarantee that things are doomed. Of course, this does leave you vulnerable and will put a strain on your relationship. If your spouse were to eventually decide that he or she no longer wanted to put up with your negativity and leaves, you would latch onto every negative thing that happened during your relationship instead of recognizing that that negativity is what drove the relationship to its end.

Fortune Telling

This cognitive distortion involves making predictions of all the bad things that could happen. Because you predict that bad things will happen, you may avoid even attempting something if you are certain you will fail. If you worry that attempting to make dinner will only result in failure anyway, you decide to save yourself the trouble or embarrassment and decide not to bother instead. The ironic part here, however, is that in refusing to attempt, you automatically confirm that your worst-case scenario happens: By refusing to attempt it, you go from having a chance of success to a 100% chance of failure just by default.

Inability to Disconfirm

In simple terms, the inability to disconfirm is the inability to accept anything you believe as wrong. It is essentially living in denial: you reject every argument or piece of evidence and have some other argument to justify any distorted thoughts. You reject the possibility that your negative thoughts may be cognitive distortions and accept them as true, even when they are not. For example, if you have the belief that you are terrible at your job if your boss ever compliments your work, you will refuse to believe it. You will instead tell yourself that it is a pity compliment, and you know that your work was subpar rather than taking the compliment at face value. No matter how hard other people will try, you will refuse to acknowledge that your own distorted beliefs even might possibly be true.

Labeling

Labeling is unproductive in general as it does nothing but call things names. Name-calling is not a viable solution for problems, nor is it healthy when rooted in negativity. When you have a core belief that uses labeling, it may look like, "I am useless," "I am unworthy," "I am a failure," or any other sort of label you have assigned yourself. By focusing on how you have labeled yourself, you will behave in ways that confirm them. For example, if you are so caught up in your label of being useless that you fail to meet your daily responsibilities, your label has essentially crippled you into being useless in that one instance. These can be more specific as well, such as, "I am a bad writer," or, "I am a horrible spouse or partner or parent or friend."

Mind Reading

Mind reading involves asserting that whatever you believe the other person is thinking is true. Usually, this is some negative thought, such as assuming that the person who looked right past you hate you, or that your friends think you are a burden because you are slower at learning something, or less skilled at a hobby than they are. You assume you know exactly what they think about you, and you act accordingly. Even though you have no way of knowing or confirming your assumptions of what others are thinking, you believe they are true.

Personalizing

Personalizing involves assuming that everything has to do with you. If your neighbor is in a bad mood, it is your fault. If your friend does not return your phone call immediately, she is mad because of something you did. If someone at the store looks angry, it is because you must have cut him off. You assume that you are to blame for everything, which is really giving yourself far more credit than deserved; most people you pass are not even aware of your existence. The world does not revolve around you, and likewise, most people are not upset because of something you did. It is unfair to you to blame yourself for everything that goes wrong for people around you. It is not your fault the person at the store is having a bad day; perhaps he is running late for an important meeting. It is not your fault that your friend did not answer the phone; she was probably busy and will get back to you eventually. It is not your fault your neighbor is in a bad mood; maybe his children have been particularly testy.

Regret Orientation

A regret orientation is when you dwell on the past. Instead of accepting that you cannot change the past, but you can learn from it to avoid making the same mistakes again, you focus instead on things you could have done differently to change the result. You do not seek to fix present or future consequences of your actions, instead choosing to look at how you could have behaved differently. This leaves you stuck with the consequences and miserable. For example, if you agreed to do something for someone, but instead got too busy and forgot, causing the other person to be upset with you understandably, you would focus on how you could have done things to ensure you remembered the project rather than how to make it up to your friend. You could have set an alarm on your phone to remind you, or made a note and put it onto your refrigerator door, or answered the phone when your friend called the night before to make sure everything was still set. Unfortunately, thinking of all the ways to fix the problem rather than the consequence means your friend will continue to be upset, and you will continue to beat yourself up about the past. This is unproductive and unreasonable, earning regret orientation a place on the list of cognitive distortions.

Unfair Comparisons

Sometimes, we look at other people and compare ourselves to them. It is easy to look at someone else and wish you had what they had. However, this is an unfair comparison; you cannot compare two entirely different situations. You did not have the same opportunities, genetic influence, lifestyle, and experiences as that other person and is unfair to yourself to compare yourself to where they are. If you see an heiress with access to a nearly bottomless trust fund, who is traveling the world, it is easy to wish you could be doing that at age 20 too, but in reality, you may have had to apply for financial aid and work two jobs just to make ends meet in college. Of course, you do not have the same experiences now. It is unfair to make yourself feel lesser due to not having the same resources. Dwelling on other people's situation is a waste of your mental energy because you do not have their situation and you will never be in exactly their situation.

Challenging Cognitive Distortions

Once you have identified which of your core beliefs are cognitive distortions, it is time to challenge them. While this can be done relatively simply, it can be tedious as it takes plenty of time before you start seeing results. The easiest way to do this is to create affirmations related to your cognitive distortions. By using affirmations, you are able to erase your core beliefs that are distorted and replace them with new ones. For example, if you have a core belief of you are unworthy of love, with the cognitive distortion of catastrophizing to reach that conclusion, you should seek to override that belief that you are unworthy of love. This takes plenty of time but can be done using a combination of affirmations and action plans, which will be covered in Strategy 10.

By creating an affirmation and utilizing it, you will begin to override the core belief. You should also take note of anything positive that shows that you are, in fact, worthy of love. Perhaps keep a journal of every time someone goes out of their way to do something nice for you, and use that to remind yourself that you are worthy of love. Remind yourself to take other people at face value when they tell you they love you. Notice how happy your friends or family get when they see you. Little by little, you will find the core belief slowly being replaced with feeling that you are, in fact, worthy of love. This process starts out difficult, but over time, it gets easier. Each success you have, every time you admit that you are loved and worthy of love will encourage you to continue moving forward on your journey.

Remember, this process works over time. It is not an instant fix, nor should you expect it to be. Keep an open mind as you begin identifying your cognitive distortions and correcting them with affirmations and action plans, and remember, this process may be uncomfortable as you force yourself to challenge beliefs you thought were a part of yourself. It is not uncommon to feel discomfort when challenging these thoughts, as you do not know what to expect when things are different. Despite feeling uncomfortable, it will be worthwhile once you get through the process.

Strategy 4: Worst Case Scenario Roleplay

As you have learned, worst case scenarios are a cognitive distortion. Especially those prone to anxiety will find themselves particularly vulnerable to their debilitating effects. It is easy for the mind to come up with a worst-case scenario when you are afraid to do something, especially if it is something important, such as choosing whether to quit a job at a secure place of employment to pursue your passion with a start-up company. It is easy for your mind to tell you that if you quit your stable job, you will fall into financial ruin, lose your house, get divorced because your spouse resents that you made a bad financial move, and ultimately, you end up homeless. Or, if you have a phobia of spiders, it is easy for your mind to justify your fear by telling yourself that the spider will bite you, you will get a rare disease, and you will ultimately die when your doctor fails to discover what the cause of your illness is.

However, as discussed, catastrophizing does nothing other than to keep you paralyzed in your own fear or anxiety. It is absolutely a distortion that you want to correct, and one of the ways to get over this form of thinking is through roleplaying. Roleplaying is when you act out how a scene would go, sort of like acting or a child playing make-believe. In this situation, you can either roleplay with yourself or with someone you would trust to discuss your mental health with. The idea is that you will imagine a scenario and what the worst case would be for how it plays out, and then roleplay through the scenario so you can see whether or not the catastrophizing was justified. This can feel difficult or uncomfortable at first, as pretending is not something adults typically do, but as you get a knack for it, you may find that it is actually a useful tool in your cognitive restructuring.

For example, imagine that you are prone to anxiety. You absolutely hate interacting with people you do not know out of fear of messing up or presenting yourself as a bumbling idiot. Because of this, you typically avoid any interaction that is not absolutely necessary, and when it is necessary, you find yourself stumbling over speaking just out of sheer nervousness. In this case, you should seek to roleplay an interaction with a cashier. Perhaps you want to order a coffee at the café, so you choose that as the setting for your roleplay.

Let us assume your best friend is there with you, acting in the part of the cashier. You walk up to your friend, who smiles at you and asks, "Welcome to Thanks a Latte Café! What can I get you today?" She waits politely for you to continue.

You pause for a moment before realizing you're frozen. "I, uh…"

"Need a minute?" your friend asks you, not really seeming to care about your deer in headlights look.

Numbly, you nod your head as you stumble to find your usual coffee preference in your racing mind. Despite your heart racing and your cheeks beginning to burn, you eventually manage to mutter out, "I'd uh... Like a small mocha...?" It could have partly been the awkwardness of the situation, or it could have been your own nerves, but saying those words out loud seemed next to impossible, and you struggled to meet your friends' gaze as you waited for her response.

"Sure! Anything else?" She seemed to ignore the awkward stuttering and shyness completely.

"N-no..." you manage to squeak out.

"Okay, that'll be $5!"

You pretend to hand her some money, and she pretends to give you a cup. The scene is over.

Despite the fact that you were anxious and shy, nothing bad happened. You were able to place your order without judgment, and even when you did freeze up or stumble over your words, nothing you were afraid of happened. No one stopped and laughed at you. You didn't get turned away. You got you to pretend coffee without any hiccups. Now, reflect on this: There was no point in getting so worked up because ultimately, the cashier does not care about whether you stumble. The cashier will likely not remember you the next time you walk through the door. By identifying the worst possible scenario that could happen, and then roleplaying through the whole scenario, you are able to see that there is no reason to catastrophize.

This can be done with no friend or family member as well, though it involves more introspection and less acting. Imagine that you are afraid of disagreeing with your significant other because you worry that you will anger or offend him so much that he refuses to continue the relationship. Because of this, you typically choose to instead defer to him no matter what to avoid any and all conflict. However, you are starting to resent the fact that you never get what you want and want to find a way to confront him as kindly and painlessly as possible.

In this situation, it could be beneficial to roleplay with roles reversed. You would imagine that your significant other is confronting you over not liking something and imagining your reaction to it. You imagine the following happening:

Your significant other approaches you, looking sheepish. "Honey, I know you really want to try out that new Thai restaurant down the street for our date night tonight, but I have to tell you. I don't really like Thai food at all. In fact, I hate it. The cilantro always makes everything taste funny, and I feel sick afterward. Can we try something else tonight, or decide to do takeout and date night at home so we can both get something we really enjoy for our special night?"

Now you imagine how you would feel during this exchange. You are certain you feel a little bit disappointed, but shrug it off and say, "That's fine! The important part about tonight is spending time with you, not going out. You go pick up takeout on your way home from work, and I'll go rent us a couple of movies we've wanted to see during my lunch break!"

You imagine your significant other looking relieved. "Really? Thanks! I'm sorry, I know this is disappointing… I just didn't want to ruin our date night at the restaurant being less than thrilled about it. I'm sorry for letting you down!"

You imagine yourself being a little perplexed at this sentiment. Why would you be annoyed or let down by your significant other voicing preferences for something as basic as food? You want to know what he likes and doesn't like so you are able to get him things he really enjoys rather than always forcing him into liking what you like.

The roleplay, at that point, is over. You have roleplayed through the other side of the situation and recognized that you would not be annoyed or upset with your significant other for voicing your preferences, so why would he be annoyed at you doing the same? Your worst-case scenario did not happen or even come close to happening. This should open your eyes a little bit more and help you see that you are being paralyzed by the worst-case scenario, but things are not nearly as scary as they may initially seem.

Your roleplays can be customized endlessly: They can involve other people or take place in your own mind with you controlling everyone. They can cover fears, insecurities, anger outbursts, and anything else that may be holding you down or causing you to look at worst cases. Ultimately, they should open your eyes to the possibility (and probability) that the worst-case scenario will not happen.

Strategy 5: Exposure Therapy

We all have various emotional triggers: There was even a journaling strategy in Strategy 1 dedicated to identifying your emotional triggers. They are so pervasive and so ambiguous that even something as simple as a child saying a certain word could become a trigger for you, or they can be as specific as feeling triggered at riding in cars on a certain road. Regardless of what the trigger is, or the severity of it, it can be useful to eliminate it over time. An effective way to do this is through exposure therapy.

Exposure therapy seeks to expose you to things that trigger you. This may seem counterproductive, as exposing you to your own emotional triggers should only cause you to react as if you have been triggered. This is true if you were, for example, terrified of spiders, so you decided that the right course of action is to go to a pet store and allow a tarantula to climb on your hand. That is going to be an extremely stressful, extremely triggering situation that will likely be bad enough to dissuade you from the process of exposure therapy completely. Contrary to what you might expect, the purpose of this is to slowly build up a tolerance to the trigger over repeated exposure in a controlled setting over time. Just like the idea that you build up a tolerance to repeated exposure to drugs like caffeine or alcohol, the idea is to build up your tolerance to your emotional trigger.

This is typically done in controlled environments, starting with the idea of your trigger and eventually working up to full exposure to whatever it is that leaves you exploding. Just like how you slowly acclimate yourself to cold water by dipping your toe, followed by your feet, followed by actually taking a step into the water, you will slowly and gently expose yourself to your trigger. By building up a tolerance, you are able to cope better in real time, avoiding awkward interactions with people who resemble your emotional triggers, or accidentally saying something hurtful that you did not mean during your fit of rage.

If your trigger response is severe, start by thinking about the concept of it. This is easiest to imagine with a phobia. If you fear spiders, imagine the sight of a spider on its web, away from you and not doing anything. Do this until the image of a spider in your mind is not immediately met with revulsion and panic.

Once you no longer panic at the thought of your trigger, try to find a representation of it somehow. If you fear spiders, you will look at photos. If angry people trigger you, look at a photo of someone in the middle of a rage. Look at the photos until you no longer feel that visceral reaction of being triggered.

After looking at photos, you should seek to watch a video of your trigger. This could be a spider actively spinning its web, or watching a recording of an angry argument from a TV show. Again, you should repeat this step until it is no longer triggering.

Next, you should seek out your trigger in real life. If yelling triggers you, find a situation in which someone is yelling at someone else. This can be staged by people you know, or it could involve legitimately just waiting to run into someone yelling at someone else. If your trigger is cars, bring yourself to a car and touch it. Maybe sit inside of it with the door shut, or even with the car turned on.

Last, you want to expose yourself to the entire trigger, uncensored. If you fear driving on the road, you should force yourself to do it. If you fear being yelled at, find someone to yell at you. You want to check that your trigger response to the stimulus has been dulled by your constant exposure to it over time. The result should be that you are able to face your trigger without some sort of outburst, even if it still makes you uncomfortable.

For example, imagine your fear being talked to in a condescending manner and frequently respond to even perceiving something as slightly condescendingly results in you flying into an uncontrollable rage. You scream and yell at the thought that someone would disrespect you in such a manner. You recognize that this disproportionate reaction to your triggers is only hurting those around you, as they are getting to the point of fearing to speak to you, worrying that your reaction will be so over the top that they walk on eggshells around you to avoid triggering you.

Recognizing that your trigger is anything that feels even remotely condescending to you, you begin your exposure therapy journey. You start by thinking about the last time someone was condescending to you: It was in a grocery store, and someone made a snarky comment about how you did not need those cookies you were eyeing in the endcap. You feel your blood begin to boil at the mere mention of the incident, clenching your fists and feeling the anger race through you. This is good! Those feelings mean you are heading in the right direction. You repeat this exercise for a few days and notice that your anger begins to fade to a minor annoyance at the implication. Now that you do not react so viscerally, it is time to move to the next step.

You decide to look up a photo of a person with a condescending smirk. His eyebrow is quirked as he smirks at you, his eyes wordlessly conveying his utter disdain for you and his own superiority. Again, you find yourself reacting strongly, immediately enraged that someone would wear that expression, even though you are looking at an inanimate photo. Just as with the previous step, you should seek to expose yourself to this step until it no longer fills you with intense rage.

You then decide it is time to watch a video. You watch a scene in a TV show that involved one character condescendingly putting down another character, who even conveniently happens to look a lot like you. You watch it and once again recognize that now-familiar bubbling of rage in your chest, though, you notice that it is not as visceral of a reaction as you once had. When the rage eventually quiets to a minor annoyance at viewing the video, you move forward.

For the sake of saving time and avoiding having to hunt down a situation that occurs uncontrolled, you seek out a friend of yours to say condescending things to another friend. He agrees to do so and proceeds to spout out as much condescending vitriol as he can think of, watching as you react. The first few times, you are enraged at the sentiment, but not nearly as strongly as before. Your friends repeat this exercise for you a few times before you decide to move to the next step.

For your last real step in exposure, you find someone that you know has always had a bit of a superiority complex and frequently puts people down with snarky asides or outright aggressive put-downs. Conveniently, you happen to work with that person. You go speak to him, and, as he usually does, he begins to speak down to you, treating you like you are dumb and incapable of learning. Much to your surprise, despite the fact that you are angry, you do not feel the same, uncontrollable rage that you used to when facing criticism or condescending words.

The beauty of this technique is that you can take it as quickly or slowly as you need to see results. Some people feel as if they will adjust to their trigger through a few repeated exposures at full intensity without any sort of gradual exposure, just as some people feel it is best to rip off the bandage or just jump into the pool without acclimating. Others will feel as if they are stuck at certain levels of exposure, or find themselves taking several weeks before the exposure to a stimulus does not trigger such awful, aggressive reactions. Ultimately, the important part of this strategy is to teach yourself to not react so emotionally to things that trigger you. The length of time it takes is not necessarily as important as the fact that you are making a conscious effort to change your life and reactions.

Strategy 6: Challenging Negative Thoughts

Negative thoughts, though similar to cognitive distortions, are slightly different. They do not always present with a cognitive distortion, but they absolutely are detrimental. It is normal for everyone to have negative thoughts at some point, whether it is a thought on how annoying it is that it is raining, or that you are angry at a company that you loved because you just found out they support a cause you are against. Humans are not programmed to think only positively, and negativity can be normal and healthy. Negative feelings are like alarm bells, warning us that something is not quite right somewhere.

Despite the fact that some negativity is absolutely normal when you are finding your thoughts plagued with negativity to the point that you feel more negative than not, you may decide it is time to take action. Negative thoughts come with physiological changes to your body, and reactions of stress. Too many negative thoughts can leave you feeling depressed, anxious, or angry at the world with no end in sight. If you feel like you are beginning to drown in negativity, it may be time to attempt challenging your negative thoughts as they arise.

This can be done in a variety of ways: You can choose to engage in cognitive restructuring, taking the tools from journaling and affirmations and using them to rewire your way of thinking through making positivity habitual in the same way negativity became habitual. You can choose to look at any negative thoughts that follow a catastrophizing mindset and challenge them through roleplay or exposure therapy. You can also try using one of the new techniques that this section will teach you.

Negative Thought Activity

This activity will have you analyze any one of your negative thoughts to decide whether or not it needs to be corrected, and if it is a thought worth thinking. Through a series of questions, you will essentially appraise your thought to decide if it serves any benefit. If it is worthless or useless, it can be discarded and ignored. There is no need to take up any precious real estate in your mind with space that will be wasted or will drag you down. You will ask yourself six questions about the thought you are questioning in order to attempt to challenge it. The examples you will encounter within each question's answer will be based upon the negative thought of, "Continuing to try to fix my situation is a waste of time and is not worth it."

Can I prove my thought with substantial evidence?

When you ask this, you provide yourself with a chance to validate your negative thought, but it has to involve things you know are a fact. You cannot use hearsay or assumptions when trying to prove your negative thought's validity. Think, as long and hard as you can about your negative thought. The person who claims to continue to try to fix his situation may answer that yes, he can prove it. By knowing that trying to fix his situation, he will fail, he is wasting his time by attempting it. That is the time that he could use in other parts of his life. Once you have answered the following questions, you will be able to think a little more clearly about the situation at hand.

Can I disprove my thought?

Just as in a formal debate, both sides get a chance to speak, you must also give disproving your negative thoughts a try. Ask yourself this question and reflect on the situation. Write anything at all that might even remotely disprove your thought, and you may be surprised to find that you can write plenty here. The person who believes continuing is useless may answer, "I gain experience through trying, even if I fail. I learn from my mistakes when I fail, so I know what not to do next time. I practiced skills that were relevant to what I was fixing. I gained familiarity with the situation." All of those statements are ways that the person may have benefitted from attempting to fix his problem, even if he knew it would ultimately fail.

Am I jumping to conclusions without seeing the whole picture?

It can be easy to jump to conclusions when presented with only part of the story. You can paint nearly any story in a positive light so long as you leave out some key details. Because it is so easy to skew your perception by not seeing the whole picture, you should ask yourself if you are jumping to conclusions. Do you feel like it is only pointless to try when you know you will fail because you really know you will fail, or because you are pretty sure you will fail, but there is a chance for success? If you are missing part of the story, you cannot make an informed decision, and likewise, if your thought is missing a significant background detail, it is likely not rational thought or feeling.

What would my friend/family member/significant other think about this thought and situation?

Asking yourself how other people would react is a fantastic way to identify a baseline for a normal reaction to a negative thought or feeling. It is sometimes easier for you to see things through someone else's eyes than it would be to see them through your own. This is because by trying to see things through someone else's eyes, you put a degree of separation between yourself and the situation. If you feel like it is useless to continue trying, would your best friend agree with you? Would your parents? What about your significant other? If any of them would think you are being overly dramatic and should try because trying at least yields a possibility of success while not trying is always going to result in failing, then maybe you should reevaluate whether your thought is worthwhile.

How does my situation change if I look at it positively instead of negatively?

Sometimes, just looking at a situation in a different light can change the entire picture. Just as different lenses in a camera will present different kinds of images, changing your perception of the situation with a positive one, even if you are not sure you actually believe it, will provide insight to whether you are thinking about things in the best way possible. If you are insistent that there is no point in trying when you will fail, then try looking at all the things you would gain through trying, even if you fail. You gain experience, wisdom, and knowledge of what not to do next time. That is already a substantial gain, even if you do not get the results you were hoping for.

Will this situation triggering my negative thought still be relevant in a year?

This is a simple question to answer. Analyze the situation and decide if it will remain relevant. If it will, your negative thought might not be entirely unfounded, as it appears to be on an important, life-changing event. If it will be irrelevant, is there really much of a point in dwelling about it? If you believe continuing to try when spiraling toward failure is useless, ask yourself if your failure will be relevant in a year. Will try to fix your problem be worthwhile in a year? Will you see any long-term benefits or consequences to attempting to succeed, but failing? Only you can answer these questions.

One Negative Thought, Two Positive Thoughts

This technique to challenging negative thoughts is a bit less nuanced than the other methods but is nonetheless effective. Every time you find yourself thinking a negative thought, you should try to drown it out with two positive ones. Positivity begets positivity, and it also is good for your health. By making sure you are consciously thinking more positive thoughts than negative, you will retrain your brain to think in positives instead of negatives. These positive thoughts can be affirmations, or they can be small positive judgments or observations, such as, "Wow, I learned a lot from that situation," or "At least I got to practice my new skill. Practice makes perfect, after all." By looking at the bright side and focusing on the positives, you will do yourself, and your mindset, a huge favor.

Strategy 7: Setting Goals

Why Set Goals?

Goal setting is a fantastic form of self-motivation. When you set goals, you give yourself something to strive for. You have something you know you want and you are able to identify that in order to have a clear idea of what your actions are for. These goals can be anything, from getting a new job to learning a skill or meeting new people. Literally, anything you would like to achieve in life can be made into a goal. Just because anything can be made into a goal does not mean that there are no guidelines, however. By following some rules, and guidelines when setting your goals, you will learn to come up with goals that will be beneficial for you and help you change your behavior or life for the better. Ultimately, your goal should offer you some sort of benefit, whether

Bad Goals

Before getting into what rules there are to rule-setting, let's first analyze what makes a goal bad. There are three types of goals you should seek to avoid, as they are not conducive to a healthy mindset, nor are they effective for the right reasons. These goals are goals seeking to be in certain emotional states, goals that focus on the past, or goals that are rooted in negativity. Each of these types of goals is poorly formed or unproductive for various reasons.

Emotional States

Oftentimes, when people are setting goals for therapy, they think, "I want to feel happy in my own body and mind." At face value, this is a fine goal, but in reality, it is deeply rooted in feelings. However, feelings are constantly changing and fluctuating. This means that your goal may be achieved some of the time, but no one is every happy with themselves all of the time. You cannot help that sometimes; you will be disappointed or angry in yourself for something you did or a way you behaved. Because of the instability of emotions, they should be avoided as goals.

Focus on the past

People frequently also decide to set their goals as, "I want to get back to my old self," especially if their symptoms they are hoping to fix came up later in life. It is not unusual to miss the person you used to be but remember, that person is in the past. That person you used to do not go through the hard times you are hoping to get yourself out of, nor did that person have the knowledge you do now. CBT seeks to focus on the present and fix your mental health issues through actions, not by seeking out the past. The past can never be made present again, and you should never try to root your goals in returning to a past relationship, a past personality, or past feelings. You will always fail.

Negative or avoidant goals

Just as affirmations have to be kept positive in order to be effective, so too do goals. While the goal of, "I want to avoid feeling depressed," might sound like a reasonable goal, all this is doing is making you hyper-focused on avoiding the feelings of depression. By focusing on avoiding rather than on fixing the distressing symptoms, you are running from your problem. You also set yourself up for failure, because any time you fail and feel depressed, you will feel that depression compound onto itself as you collect another piece of evidence that you are as worthless and helpless as you thought you were. Ultimately, it is best to avoid setting goals with a focus on negativity or avoidance and instead focus on goals that are active instead.

SMART Goals

Now that you understand what not to do with your goals, it is time to learn what good goals consist of. It helps to remember that SMART goals are the most effective goals, with SMART being an acronym for specific, measurable, attainable, relevant, and timely. If you remember this acronym, you will be able to make your goals work for you.

Specific

When setting your goal, you want to be as specific with what you wish to attain as possible. The more specific you are, the clearer the picture you paint in your mind of what you want to achieve. There is a huge difference between saying you want to paint your room blue instead of specifying that you specifically want a light cerulean color, and likewise, there is a difference between saying you want to manage feelings of anger and angry outbursts, and stating that you want to reduce your outbursts over the course of the month. You went from a somewhat specific goal to one that gave an exact picture of what it will be.

Measurable

Just as more specific goals are desirable, having goals that are easily measurable is also crucial to set a good, productive goal. You need to be able to quantify what success looks like so you know exactly when you reach it, whether that is stating that you will write a certain amount of words a day, or save a certain amount of money. In the example of wanting to reduce anger outbursts, you could specify that you want to reduce the total number of times you react in anger by 40%. This goal now has a quantifiable definition of success.

Attainable

Your goal needs to be something you can actually reasonably complete. The easiest way to do this is to make sure your goal can easily be broken down into smaller goals to keep you motivated and moving forward. Every time you meet a goal, you feel encouraged, which keeps you moving forward, striving to complete more of your goals. This positive feedback loop reinforces the idea of meeting your goals, motivating you to start in the first place once your body and mind realize that doing so can be both beneficial and enjoyable. For example, if you set a goal of reducing angry outbursts, specifying smaller goals may make it more realistic for you to complete. You could say that you want to make it a point to have one less angry outburst than you did the day before every day. This gives you small milestone goals that will help keep you on track to attaining the whole goal.

Realistic

By making sure your goal is realistic, you avoid setting yourself up for failure. A realistic goal for one person is not going to be the same as a realistic goal for another; a fit, experienced mountain climber may be able to set and achieve a goal of climbing a huge mountain with a month to prepare, but the vast majority of people who do not mountain climb on a regular basis would likely find themselves falling out. Likewise, it can be realistic for one person to go running every day, but someone paralyzed from the neck down will never be able to attain it. Make sure your goal is reasonable and realistic to your specific situation. If you want to alleviate your anger issues and stop having angry outbursts, you have to set a realistic goal that recognizes that the process of changing your habits and mindsets.

Timed

Defining how long your goal will take gives you a clear goal with an end in sight. You give yourself a time to complete the goal by, and anything beyond that is deemed a failure. Keep in mind that you should give yourself a reasonable amount of time to complete your goal. Be realistic about your timeline and make sure it has at least some leeway for you to complete it while still giving yourself time as a motivator to work toward it. For example, if you want to reduce your angry outbursts, you decide on one month for the timeline to begin to see a reduction of 30%.

Examples of Goals

With an understanding of what a goal needs to be SMART, you will be ready to set goals that are beneficial to your mental wellbeing. Here are a few examples of goals. Try to identify whether they are SMART and if they are not, fix them to make them SMART.

- *I will pass my class this quarter with at least a B average.*
- *I will exercise three days a week so I can lose five lbs. before summer*
- *I will read more.*
- *I will get a new job.*
- *I will save 10% of my paychecks every week, so I can buy a car by December.*
- *I will cut how often I have panic attacks in half by February.*

Strategy 8: Mindful Meditation

Mindfulness is one of those concepts that people struggle to define. We will consider mindfulness a way of focusing your attention on the present moment, specifically seeking to detach any sort of emotional feelings to your observations. Ideally, you will be able to take a step back from what is happening to you and look at it calmly and without attachment, with the goal being that you can recognize your feelings for what they are without falling into destructive behaviors or habits. By disconnecting from your emotions while identifying what is happening to you and how you are feeling, you are able to control yourself or recognize that your emotions are causing you to act irrationally or destructively

Achieving mindfulness is the hardest part of this technique, as it can be incredibly difficult to separate yourself from your emotions if you are untrained or unaccustomed to doing so. However, this does not mean it has to be impossible for you! You can learn how to achieve mindfulness through meditation and relaxation. By doing so, you will be able to return to a state of mindfulness any time you notice your control over your emotions starting to slip. This is yet another action you can take to prevent yourself from engaging in thoughts, feelings, or behaviors that you wish to change.

The easiest way to heighten your awareness to your feelings and to disengage from the overwhelming feelings and thoughts is through a sort of meditation as soon as you begin to feel out of control. This grounding technique involves identifying things around you that you can engage with each of your senses. Doing so will help you return to a state of calmness, in which you will be able to begin identifying your true feelings or actions so you can take steps to stop before you spiral any further.

First, focus on five things around you can see. Really focus on each of the things you see, taking in their details and take deep, slow breaths. Look at the texture of the fabric, the way the fur on that dog almost ripples in the wind, or just how blue the sky looks above you at that moment. Describe the things you see to yourself as you continue to breathe slowly. You should begin to feel the sense of powerless and lack of control begin to wane.

Touch four things, running your fingers over their surfaces and focus on the texture. Is the fabric soft, plush, or rough? Smooth and satiny? Is it warm or cold? As you draw your attention away from the emotions swirling around inside your mind, you feel yourself gaining more control over yourself. Your breaths, actions, and thoughts are deliberate as you continue this process.

Listen for three distinct sounds you can discern around you. Hear the soft trill of the birds outside, singing to the morning. Are they high-pitched and melodious, or are they harsher, like the caw of a crow? Can you hear the low rumble of cars driving down the road? If you are in a quieter setting, can you hear your own breathing? Is it quick or slow? Labored or relaxed? Focus on the details, paint yourself a picture of what you can hear, and feel your stress melt away as you focus less on your stressors and more on your environment.

Next, identify two things that you can smell. Is there food cooking in the background? What about the light floral sweetness of your laundry soap on your clothes around you? Whatever the smell is, try to describe it. Is it sweet or sour? Is it pleasant? Spicy? Whatever it is, make a note of it and move to the final step.

Lastly, you should identify one thing that you can taste. Is the faint hint of the spices from lunch still present in your mouth? Maybe you are currently chewing on gum. Or perhaps, one of the scents you identified in the previous step is so strong that you can taste them on the air.

Once you have completed these steps, notice that you are firmly grounded once more. Your heartbeat should slow, and you should return to a state of relative control. Now, you are prepared to use your newfound mindfulness to change your actions, making healthier, more productive choices that will not worsen your situation.

Imagine that you have intense anxiety. You know you have to go take an important exam, and just the thought of tests usually makes you nervous. They are stressful and always trigger your anxiety. You get so caught up in the fact that you are being tested that you frequently do horribly, wasting most of your time crippled by the anxiety over failing, which only makes your anxiety worse than it already was.

You walk into the room to take the exam, surrounded by other people there for the same purpose. Immediately, you feel your blood pressure spike. Your body feels icy cold, and your heart is racing. You can hardly think because you are so anxious about failing. You take your exam and go sit down at your seat, staring at the page as you realize that you are so stressed out, you can hardly focus on the words in front of you. Rather than panicking, even more, you remember to use your mindfulness training and the 5-4-3-2-1 rule.

You identify the various things around you and feel the sensation of panic slowly ebb away, leaving yourself detached from your panic just enough to get through to the rational part of your mind. Repeat some affirmations to yourself to gain control of the situation now that the sensation of panic is gone. Remind yourself that you are safe and okay and that taking the test is not the end of the world. Quickly work through the worst-case scenario of what would happen even if you failed the test. At worst, your grade for the class is lower, but you know that it will be high enough that you at the very least pass. Use the skills you have been developing throughout this book to work past your fear of the situation and take the exam without the sensation of panic distracting you.

Ultimately, this method is especially useful when your emotions are out of your control. They will ground you and reach out to the rational part of your mind, which up until that point, had been drowned out by your emotional part. The emotional part of your brain demanded so much attention and focus, that you were unable to hear the rational part in the back, whispering to you that you may have been over-reacting, or that you could do something simple to regain control over the situation. You become so focused on the emotional part that it is difficult to listen to anything else. Remember this strategy for returning to a baseline of neutral so you can use it in conjunction with other techniques to solidify the changes you seek to make to your life.

Strategy 9: Thought-Feeling-Action Charts

As the first section of this book emphasized, the most basic concept in CBT is the relationship between thoughts, feelings, and actions. Your thoughts influence your feelings, which influence your actions, which, in turn, once again influence your thoughts. It is an endless cycle, and typically, once the cycle has begun, it is left to play out endlessly unless you disrupt it somehow. While disrupting a single part is one way to alter it, another is to identify the cycle, and then create a new one, where all three parts are changed at once. This means that you will have a new way of thinking and a new plan for your actions, so you are consciously changing multiple parts of the cycle instead of just one. This technique has two parts: Identifying the current cycle and creating a new cycle.

Identifying your Thought-Feeling-Action Cycles

The easiest way to begin this process is to spend your day tracking your feelings. Every time you feel a strong feeling, or as soon as you can after the fact, you should write down how you felt. This can be anything: Angry, happy, disappointed, annoyed, etc. The point here is to be as specific as possible, and if it takes more than a few words to describe it, that is okay. We do not always have a word for the feelings we experience, but try to get as close to what you felt as possible onto paper for future reference. For example, imagine you work at a salon as a hair stylist. You felt annoyed earlier because your 4:00pm appointment did not show up, and you had turned away another client just prior to that because you wanted to be available for the appointment that had been made out of principle. That potential client instead went to one of your coworkers and asked for a cut, color, and style job, which you know usually bring in a larger pay, and also lead to larger tips. By turning down that job and having the client who had booked an appointment not show up, you were left without any work to do, and you had lost potential money. You should write down what you felt annoyed and disappointed.

Then, identify the resulting behavior. Perhaps a client was walking in for another appointment right as you threw down your scissors angrily onto your tray. You did not mean any harm, but you could not help it; your anger at the situation was overwhelming, and throwing the scissors at the metal tray seemed like the least destructive action out of everything you wanted to do. Just as your scissors clanged against the tray, you made eye contact with another walk-in. The client looks at you, then quickly goes over to another stylist, preferring to trust her hair and the integrity of her scalp to someone who is not so angry, they are throwing sharp instruments around. When writing down the action that happened as a result of your feelings, you should write down that you scared away another potential customer by throwing a pair of scissors.

Now, you should seek to identify your thoughts that had occurred right as you were angered by the client not showing up for the appointment. In this case, you felt annoyed and frustrated that you had lost out on potential income. Notice that after throwing the scissors, you lost out on yet another potential client and more potential income. Your thoughts of negativity became self-fulfilling, and your outburst cost you even more money than you originally would have been losing. This is the problem with negative thought-feeling-behavior charts; they reaffirm themselves and leave you trapped in a constant negative cycle that you struggle to ever break free from if you do not understand how to do so.

Creating New Thought-Feeling-Action Cycles

Thankfully, there are ways of disrupting this cycle. You can seek to use affirmations to change your thoughts. You can use action plans, which will be discussed in Strategy 10, to change your behaviors. However, by creating an entirely new thought-feeling-action cycle, you will be able to alter both your thoughts and your actions at the same time by planning out how you will react as well as correcting the thought process that caused the negative feelings in the first place.

Imagine the same scenario you just went through. You have a chart that says that you thought you had wasted your time and lost money, which made you feel angry, which caused you to throw the scissors and scared off another potential client, which made you feel like you had wasted your time and lost even more money. With that cycle written in front of you, you can begin to identify how you can alter the cycle. Underneath your previous cycle that you identified, draw three big circles or squares in the shape of a triangle. There should be one at the top, with space to write in, with two underneath it. Place an arrow pointing from the top to the bottom right space, then from the bottom right to the bottom left, and from the bottom left to the top space. This will represent your cycle.

In the bottom left square, write how you could have changed your behavior or acted in a more positive manner. Perhaps you could have instead taken three deep breaths and reminded yourself that you did the right thing by waiting for your client. You could have chosen to avoid an outburst and worked toward keeping your temper under control. You could have reminded yourself of your goal to reduce the number of outbursts you have or recited a few of your affirmations. Ultimately, you decide to write down, "I could have taken a deep breath and recited my affirmations."

Next, write how doing that would have changed your thought processes over the entire situation. Imagine how those actions would have made you feel after going through them. Perhaps, after taking your deep breaths and reciting affirmations, you think that you were able to overpower your impulse to behave angrily and remind yourself that you are capable of controlling your emotions. By being levelheaded and professional, you affirm that you are a good worker, and you know that there will be other opportunities to make money later.

Lastly, you identify how those thoughts would have changed your feelings. You realize that you would have felt proud, confident, and in control. You had just succeeded in accomplishing something you had been trying to do, and despite the adversity, you are thrilled that you managed to control yourself and leave a good impression on those around you.

This skill is beneficial for after-the-fact corrections of your behavior. By seeing how the positive action would have changed things, you become more attached to the idea of using these positive actions in real time rather than using your bad habits of resorting to anger or losing control. As you adjust to using positive methods, you find your anger getting more and more under control.

Strategy 10: Create an Action Plan

When in school, children are made to go through drills of what to do in the event of a fire. They go through fire drills, earthquake drills, inclement weather drills, and even lockdown drills. Children are taught to practice stop, drop, and roll if they ever find themselves on fire, and are taught what to say to strangers that approach them. These plans are rehearsed, so children know what to do when caught in the moment. Without a plan in place, they might not know what to do, or they may freeze up, leading them to waste valuable time they could use to escape a situation unscathed. Likewise, when you are approached with an uncomfortable or volatile situation, it can be easy to react emotionally instead of rationally, which can oftentimes only inflame the issue more. Luckily, you have the opportunity of creating action plans so you have a plan to default to when a triggering situation arises.

What Makes a Good Action Plan?

Not all action plans are good or productive. In fact, you can create an action plan that is actually completely unproductive and negative. In order to be a good action plan, it must be positive or neutral, beneficial, and working toward behavioral goals you have set for yourself. This means that your action plan must generally be a positive behavior. This means that it has no negative repercussions to doing so. It must be productive, meaning that it is an action that does something, as opposed to being based in inaction. It must also help you achieve a better mental state than the one you started with.

How to Make an Action Plan

Making an action plan is not as complicated as it seems. You should start by identifying a situation that you know triggers you. This can be anything: Test anxiety, arguing with someone, or even interviewing for a job are all possible emotional triggers. Let's continue as if you are a person who struggles with arguing. Any time you perceive someone as arguing with you, you immediately become angry, overly aggressive in your speech patterns, and become intimidating in general. You identify arguing as your emotional trigger and decide to make an action plan for the next time you feel as if someone has picked a fight with you.

First, you must think of a behavior that will be positive. If you think someone is picking an argument, arguing back does nothing more than making the situation worse. It is unproductive at best and outright inflammatory at its worst. In this situation, maybe you choose not to argue. This is neutral; it does not lead to the argument getting worse and does not escalate the situation while adding no benefit. However, inaction is not a productive activity, so this is not an acceptable solution.

Instead, you decide to take a more active approach and take three deep breaths to give yourself a moment to analyze the situation and decide whether or not the other person is actually picking an argument. This is more effective than before, as you take a moment to think logically and disconnect from your anger. Now, you have chosen behavior that is positive, as stopping and taking a few deep breaths benefits you by helping you calm down and think rationally. It is active, meaning you are actually doing something that can change the situation. In this case, the action is calming yourself down rather than expending energy, arguing back with the other person. It also is beneficial to bettering your mindset and situation, meaning you will leave the situation better than you entered it. In this case, calming down allows you to avoid the entire argument altogether, leaving you calmer and happier.

With your new action plan in place, you go out about your day as usual. Toward the end of the day, a client at work decides to argue with you about a discount he insists he qualifies for, but the computer is saying he does not. You immediately feel the desire to snap back that you know your job, you are competent and fully capable, but if he does not think so, he is more than welcome to leave. You open your mouth to let your tirade out but remember your action plan. Instead, you close your mouth, take a few deep breaths, and re-evaluate the situation. Yes, the client is rude, but ultimately you know your company better than he does and there is no reason for you to argue to prove it.

Instead of continuing to argue, you tell him you will take care of his problem right away, and refuse to engage in the argument. He even repeats himself a few more times, as if you had not heard him the first time, and every time you feel your anger returning, you take another deep breath and remind yourself to stay calm. Within a few minutes, you solve his problem and send him on his way. You avoided an argument that could have gotten you in trouble with your boss, and you proved the client wrong without stooping to his level and fighting.

Benefits of Action Plans

Action plans have all sorts of benefits when used successfully. They can leave you feeling less anxious, as you know exactly how you will handle a certain situation you may fear when it arises. They can leave you feeling prepared to handle emotional triggers that used to paralyze you. They can help you build a safety plan in situations that would usually cause you to lash out at others. No matter what well-formed action plan you start with, you will find plenty of benefits to seeing it through, and the results will be undeniable. By planning out your reaction and being prepared, you are able to handle better any issues you may encounter. You feel more confident because you handled the situation in a productive manner, leaving you feeling proud of yourself and reinforcing the benefit of not reacting emotionally.

After reinforcing the benefit of your action plan, you will be more likely to continue using it in other aspects of your life. Just as when a child learns that asking please in one context usually yields positive results, so they extrapolate to using it everywhere, you will see the benefit in creating more and more action plans. Quickly, you find the use of action plans in more areas of your life than you ever expected, and you are reaping the benefits of being prepared for whatever life throws your way.

Strategy 11: Self-Care

Oftentimes, one of the best ways to improve your patience for coping is to make sure that you are providing yourself with the care you need. It is easy to forget to care for yourself when you are so caught up in life, or when you feel as if you are undeserving of basic care. However, when you are not maintaining yourself, you will not have the patience or energy to handle when life throws you a curveball because you have invested so much of your emotional energy elsewhere. Your emotional battery, so to speak, is either already depleted, or close to being depleted, and you will need to fill it somehow. You are deserving of care, no matter how strongly you feel otherwise; everyone deserves to be able to rest and enjoy themselves sometimes.

What Self-Care Entails

There are plenty of ways you can engage in this self-care, and it will look different for every individual person. The important part is that this self-care works to make you a healthier person in some way, shape, or form. The self-care also needs to be enjoyable for you; just as when you diet, you want to enjoy your food, you should enjoy the process of becoming a healthier person overall and when engaging in self-care. There are four major types of self-care that this book will address, and all of them are important to make a person who is overall a healthy individual, not just physically, but mentally as well. You may add other aspects of your life that you desire to provide yourself with self-care in, such as spiritual or work-place, but these will not be addressed in this book. Remember to follow the pattern of doing something that will make you healthier in those areas of your life, and you will be able to add those categories to your list as well.

Physical Self-Care

Physical self-care involves actions that keep your body healthy and in a condition that allows you to get through your day-to-day obligations. It is important for you to maintain your body, as it is the only one you have! You have to cherish it and recognize it as valuable, even if that is difficult for you. Some ways you can care for your body include the following:

- Get enough sleep and keep your schedule regular
- Eat primarily healthily
- Take a walk or get some form of exercise daily
- Rest when your body needs it (i.e. you are sick or injured)
- Eat all of your meals when you are hungry

Psychological Self-Care

Psychological self-care includes activities that help you remain level-headed and engaged enough in the world around you to address any challenges that come your way. These are, in a sense, ways you care for yourself that keep you sane. Just because you cannot see when your mind needs some care the way you can see when your body does, does not give you an excuse to neglect your psychological health. Some ways you can care for your mind include:

- Keep journals
- Ask for advice or guidance from someone you trust or who knows the situation better than you do
- Relax at least once a day
- Leave your work at work and disengage from work responsibilities when you are home (i.e., turn off your work phone and disable work email notifications)
- Get a hobby, and do it regularly

Emotional Self-Care

Emotional self-care is somewhat different from psychological self-care. It involves providing yourself an environment in which you are safe to feel your emotions, no matter how positive or negative. You deserve to feel emotionally supported, and these are some suggestions to ensure that you do:

- Create a gratitude journal
- Do something nice for yourself each day
- Create friendships in which you can speak honestly about how you are doing.
- Find groups of people that enjoy similar hobbies, such as a book club or a hobby sports group local to you
- Seek out support groups if you are recovering from trauma or trying to cope with something difficult

Relationship Self-Care

This type of self-care keeps you maintaining relationships with others. This is about encouraging friendships that you are secure in, and also maintaining positive relationships with coworkers. On the other hand, it is also about knowing that it is okay to let go of relationships that are toxic to you, or that you do not desire to be in. Some ways to practice relationship self-care include:

- Prioritize the most important relationships above all others, such as with spouses, children, or immediate family.
- Make an effort to be available to those you love on a regular basis
- Set aside time to spend quality time with your loved ones
- Always attend the special events of your loved ones, such as weddings, birthdays, or other important occasions
- Let go of relationships that are toxic to you, and only foster the ones that make you happy or that you feel secure within

Create a Self-Care Plan

Now that you understand the different aspects of your life that require self-care, you are ready to begin planning one. Take a piece of paper and write down the four categories: Physical, Psychological, Emotional, and Relationships. Under each of these categories, you should write at least one way you will engage in self-care, but more is advised. The more ways you engage in self-care, the better condition your body will be in. Make sure that every self-care act you engage in is one that is legitimately enriching to you and that you will enjoy.

Look at the list you have created, and commit it to memory. You want to ensure that you are confident that you will engage in these steps and that you are committed to engaging in them. Once you have it memorized, tape it up somewhere you will see it regularly. You could type it up onto a sticky note on your computer, or literally tape up the paper on your mirror, so you see it every time you wash your hands or get ready to go somewhere. You want it somewhere that you will regularly see in order to remind you that it is there and encourage you to move forward with the activities.

Next, you need to make it a point to engage in these activities regularly. You need to care for your body and mind over time in order to see results. While one day here and there will not completely derail your progress, when you are spending more days not engaging in self-care than you are, you are likely not going to see much of an improvement in your life. This is an important step to repairing your mental well-being, and you owe it to yourself to ensure you care for yourself, as no one has as much of a vested interest in making sure you are well then you do.

After a month, you should stop and reassess your situation. Record how far you have come, and acknowledge areas of your life that have been improved. Just as you will not lose a drastic amount of weight in a month, you will not see huge changes after one month of self-care, but the ones that are there should be noticeable, at least to you. Remember, these plans and actions may take upwards of a month before they become habits, so you need to remember to be realistic with your expectations. Check again in three months and record your progress. This is when you should start seeing big improvements in your attitude, behaviors, and a general sense of wellness, especially when pairing this self-care with the other methods of CBT. Remember to remain patient and realistic as you see progress, and keep up with building the habits. It will get easier with time, and you will see results that are worth the effort.

Strategy 12: Find a Good Therapist

Sometimes, no matter how hard you try, you find yourself unable to fix your own problems. You are too stuck in your head, or you find it too hard to continue past correcting and challenging your cognitive distortions. You cannot make progress you desire, even with instruction provided in this book. This is okay! Some people are not able to make it through the process on their own and need extra support. You can still get through this, even if it is not by yourself. No one will look at you as lesser for admitting you need help. If you do need help, the next step is to find a good therapist, trained in CBT, who can help you through the process. These people literally go to school for years to learn how to help those who need extra support to find their way back to mental wellness. There is a huge demand for people in this field, so you should find no shortage of therapists available to you.

Just because therapists are available, however, does not mean that they are necessarily good, or that they would be a good match for you. Sometimes, people have to go through three or four different therapists before they find a match for them. Do not feel discouraged if you do not click with the first one you make an appointment with, or if it takes you a while to feel comfortable going to therapy. This is a process that is often difficult for people. It is not easy to tell yourself that you need help in a way that you cannot provide yourself, and it is not easy to open up to other people and make yourself as vulnerable as you will be to a therapist. Remind yourself that the process will be worth the effort and discomfort if you need to and tell yourself that your mind deserves the clarity and wellbeing that this process will provide you.

Qualities of a Good Therapist

Good therapists have a wide variety of skills at their disposal, as well as the intricate knowledge of the psychology field and the experience necessary to guide their clients through the process of reaching mental wellness. Knowledge alone is not enough: Certain skills will make for a more effective therapist, and more effective means less time spent wading through the process. When you first go in for an appointment or consultation, you should make a decision within the first session or two on whether you want to continue. Here is a list of traits that make for effective therapists that you should look out for:

Empathetic

An empathetic therapist will be understanding of what you are going through while maintaining the topic of the conversation or session on you. They are reassuring and warm in their interactions with you and accept what you are saying without judgment. This leaves you feeling like your therapist is genuinely interested in hearing what you have to say and that your therapist truly does care about you.

Trustworthy

Trust is the most important part of your relationship with your therapist, and if you do not immediately feel as if they are trustworthy, they are most likely not right for you. If you cannot trust your therapist implicitly, you will struggle to open up and be honest about issues that matter, and this lack of honesty will hinder your progress. When you do trust your therapist, however, you know that you can speak without judgment and know that, ultimately, your therapist wants to help you get better.

Professional

Your therapist, while he or she should be warm and empathetic, must also maintain a degree of professionalism. You should not have to worry about your therapist's feelings during a session, nor should you find yourself comforting him or her after something you have said. Your therapist should be able to distance his or her own reaction to information or traumas you have experienced, even if they bring up strong emotions. Those emotions should be firmly locked away somewhere you will never see. The focus of these sessions is on you.

Fosters a feeling of partnership

In a therapeutic relationship, it is important for you to feel as if you and your therapist are partners. This enables you to be willing to open up to the therapist and allows you to rely on him or her in the ways necessary when engaging in therapy. If you do not feel as if you could be partners with your therapist, then that is not the right one for you.

Flexible

Flexibility is absolutely necessary when trying to heal invisible wounds. Your therapist needs to be able to go with the flow, and even though CBT is a structured therapy, not every person is the same. He or she needs to be able to adjust expectations, plans, topics, and coping mechanisms specifically to you in order to be effective.

Effective communicator

Being able to understand what your therapist is saying is crucial to understanding what you should be doing to recover. Your therapist should be good enough at communicating that he or she can take complicated psychological processes and break them down into normal speech that is uncomplicated and easily understood. Without being able to do so, your therapist will not be able to instruct you.

Committed

When you are signing up for therapy, you are going to naturally gravitate toward the therapists that seem committed to their jobs. You want someone who genuinely enjoys the process of aiding other people and not someone who is burnt out and not very committed to doing a good job. If you get the sense that your therapist is uncommitted, or uninterested in the position in general, you may want to seek a new therapist.

Inspiring

Lastly, a good therapist is inspiring. He or she should inspire you to want to better yourself. His or her words should keep you motivated, and you should leave your appointments inspired to continue working toward your goals. A therapist that does not inspire you on a personal level will not inspire you to make the difficult changes you will need to finish your process.

How to Find and Choose a Therapist

With an understanding of what traits to look for and which to avoid, you are ready to begin your search for a therapist. The easiest way to do this will probably be by calling your insurance and asking which in your area are covered under your benefits, but you can also do a local search to find any other therapists. Your primary care doctor can also provide you with a referral to therapists if your insurance requires it. Be open with him or her about the mental health issues you are having so your doctor can refer you to the best possible therapist for your situation.

Once you have your list of therapists in your area or a referral, it is time to prepare for your first appointment. You should create a list of questions for points that are important or relevant for you to understand where your therapist stands on a wide range of issues that may come up in your sessions. For example, if you are LGBTQ, you may want to know if your therapist can accept that, or if any personal biases could make that process difficult. If you are non-religious, you may want to ask if the therapist has any religious biases that will interfere with the process. If you are struggling with a toxic family, you may want to question whether the therapist would ever consider ending a relationship with a family member as an option.

When you get to your first appointment, pay special attention to your feelings toward the therapist. Take any reactions you have at face value, and if you feel anything is off for any reason, or you feel as if you will not click with the therapist, it is completely acceptable and within your right to try a new one. Remember your list of qualities that make for an effective therapist and check them off in your mind as you decide which the one in front of you encompasses. Ultimately, you need to have a comfortable, trust-based relationship with your therapist to be able to truly better your situation, and if you feel as if that would not happen for any reason, try to find another. Even if you are struggling to find a therapist in your area, there are now multiple options for online or distance therapy sessions where your sessions take place over a webcam rather than in an office. This is an option if you do not click with any of the therapists around you, or if you do not have regular access to a therapist in your area.

By keeping in mind what traits make for an effective therapist and understanding what kind of person you need to be able to trust, you will be able to make the best, the most informed decision you can when choosing a therapist. Through some effort, and a little bit of luck, you will find a therapist that will be best equipped to guide you through your process to mental wellness.

CONCLUSION

Congratulations—you have made it to the end of *CBT Made Simple: 12 Practical Strategies to Overcome Depression, Anger, and Anxiety and Finally Manage Your Worries*. This book has provided you with the basic information you will need to understand CBT, as well as 12 strategies to overcoming mental health issues. Each of the techniques provided in this book can be combined, and all of them work together to create one comprehensive effect: shifting your negative thoughts into positive ones to alter your behavior for good. By following these processes and remaining determined, you will be able to see a drastic difference in yourself before and after attempting CBT. The insight this book will provide you will be invaluable to anyone, regardless of whether you struggle with mental health issues or not. Anyone can better their life through this process, and they can make positive ripples into waves in their life if they commit themselves to do so.

Now that you have been provided this knowledge, it is up to you what you do with it. You are armed with everything you will need to begin the reprogramming process. The important key to remember is that you must remain vigilant, diligent, and persistent, even when things get tough. Despite being simple, no one said this process was easy, and taking on the task of rewiring your brain is a gargantuan one to take.

Remember, even if you feel yourself slipping back into your old, negative ways, you can stop yourself and remind yourself of the good that comes with productive, adaptive behaviors. No matter how far you fall, it is never too late to get back up and keep moving forward. Your positivity is infectious, and it will spread throughout your life like wildfire. Your habits that once seemed impossible to change will become forgotten, discarded in favor of productive behaviors that benefit not only you but those around you as well. The important part is that you continue to try, even when it seems impossible, and even when staring your negative thoughts in the eye, you persevere. You can defeat your negativity, so long as you are willing to put in the effort.

You are worthy of creating a life in which you are happy, comfortable, and loved. You deserve to be happy, free from anxiety or depression. You deserve never to feel that loss of control that comes with being emotionally triggered, and you deserve to be armed with the knowledge and skills you will need to take on your negative thoughts. Remember, slow and steady wins the race, and you will win this one by removing negative thoughts, one-by-one, no matter how tedious or difficult the task may seem. You are strong enough to succeed, and one day, you will look back at this difficult time in your life and realize that you had the strength inside you all along.

Was this book helpful? your review on Amazon is important to me! thank you!

CPSIA information can be obtained
at www.ICGtesting.com
Printed in the USA
FSHW010705190120
66258FS

9 781075 388989